WOMAN AT HOME

WOMAN
AT HOME

Arlene Rossen Cardozo

DOUBLEDAY & COMPANY, INC.
GARDEN CITY, NEW YORK
1976

During the past several years, many women from various parts of the country have contributed their thoughts, attitudes, feelings, and information on their particular life styles to this book. To protect the privacy of all those who were generous enough to share of themselves in this way, the identities of persons quoted in the book have been changed.

Library of Congress Cataloging in Publication Data
Cardozo, Arlene.
  Woman at home.

  1. Housewives—United States. 2. Mothers. 3. Self-actualization (Psychology) I. Title.
HQ759.C287   301.42'7
ISBN: 0-385-11674-8
Library of Congress Catalog Card Number: 75-40717

To
Mother and *Daddy*
and to
Dick, Miriam, Rachel, and *Rebecca*

Acknowledgments

This book could not have been written without the tremendous amount of encouragement, faith, and reason my husband Dick gave to the whole undertaking.

I am also deeply indebted to many friends and colleagues, particularly to: Sharon Wikstrom, for her constant moral support, and for the invaluable comments she made on each draft of the manuscript; Marge Roden, for her sound professional advice and judgments; Nancy Conroy, for her sensitive thoughts and opinions; Kathy O'Conner, for her long-distance telephone transfusions of enthusiasm; and Helen DuPont, for bringing with her on each visit from Washington new reasons why a book about women at home had to be written.

I'm also very grateful to my sister, Ricky Weiss, for her ideas and strong personal support; to my Aunt Ro Rossen, for her suggestions; and to our daughters, Miriam, Rachel, and Rebecca, for their inspiration and their help.

A.R.C.

Contents

Foreword

The woman who elects to stay at home to raise her family has received little social support for her decision during the past decade. Major spokespersons for and about women have been those feminists whose energies are directed to altering the age-old norm that every woman should marry, have children, and stay at home to raise them. Their efforts have resulted in changes for the unmarried woman, the married childless woman, and for the woman who chooses to work outside home in addition to raising her family. The single woman is now viewed as a woman who elects a particular option, rather than as a woman who couldn't get a man. The childless married woman is regarded as one who chooses marriage but not family. The married woman who works outside home is not considered a negligent mother, but rather a woman who has opted for a certain way of life.

Feminism has helped to free the single woman, the childless married woman, and the working mother for jobs outside home without sex bias and for pursuit of their choices without stigma. But feminist spokespersons, in their zeal to create an alternative view, have established—intentionally or unintentionally—a position antithetical to a woman's staying at home to raise her family.

Out of necessity, perhaps, the first decade of modern feminism had to dedicate itself to creating a new norm: that a woman must feel a sense of self-worth and accomplishment about what she does; that these feelings could be achieved through escaping the stereotype that every woman marry, and stay at home to raise a family; that even the married woman with children could escape the stereotype by taking a job outside home.

We now risk replacing the old norm with a new one. It is as damaging for our society to enforce the expectation that every woman must work outside home in order to achieve feelings of self-worth and accomplishment as it was to perpetuate the myth that a woman could derive "fulfillment" only through marrying and having children.

If we are to prevent substituting one crushing, myopic view for another, we must work toward true life-style alternatives for women. Among these alternatives is a woman's choice to marry, have children, and (when financially possible) to stay at home to raise them. We must direct as much energy to supporting the validity of this woman's option as to the options of the woman who does not make this choice.

WOMAN AT HOME is written in full support of the woman who chooses to stay at home to raise her family. It is directed to the particular needs and concerns of the woman who wishes to keep her family in primary focus and pursue personal interests without leaving home.

WOMAN AT HOME

Introduction:
Beyond Feminism

Why, in this age of modern feminism, does an intelligent, thinking woman stay at home to raise her family rather than go out to work? To appreciate why the woman at home makes this choice, one must first analyze the context from which modern feminism emerged and then investigate the discrepancy between feminist theory and the realities faced by mothers who choose to work away from home.

Modern feminism arose in the wake of the Second World War, as the Western world was enjoying material wealth and suffering spiritual poverty. God had been proclaimed dead then, and was replaced by an atheistic cry of despair uttered by the nihilists of the French cafés, most notably Jean-Paul—Man Is in Anguish—Sartre and the exponent of the New Womanhood, Simone de Beauvoir, whose book *The Second Sex* predated contemporary American feminist writings. De Beauvoir had much to tell women—theoretically—about their lives, and though she herself chose neither marriage nor family, she greatly influenced women who had chosen both. Among them was Betty Friedan, whose book *The Feminine Mystique*, published in 1963, provided impetus for the women's liberation movement in this country. Friedan's book had tremendous impact upon married women with families who believed themselves left out of the mainstream of life. Many of these women were, in fact, bystanders at a great race nowhere.

Among the racers were absentee husbands, who, consumed by an ethic which dictated constant work as the means of success, had abandoned their wives and children, physically and emotionally, as they worked long hours, nights, and weekends to provide a variety of "important" things—among them status (derived from jobs which kept the family separated, and often moving) and money (to buy substitutes for what was really needed: time and attention). With extended-family ties weakened and old friends scattered, loneliness became a way of life, as the success ethic, which assumes the way to *get* ahead is to *move* ahead, produced a generation of mobile nuclear families.

Left at the helm were women, equipped with varying degrees of education and work experience, but unprepared for the feelings of total abandonment they felt. Away in many instances from extended families, raising children far from anyone whose mores were familiar, women were thrust into a lonely abyss. Friends and family were gone, husbands were gone, and out in the bedroom suburbs women existed with only their children and each other to talk to. The normal age span when infants and grandparents lived side by side was replaced by a society of young mothers and young children—older mothers lived with their teen-agers in another part of a suburb a step up the ladder. Life seemed hollow and void.

Women's liberation, which originated as an attempt to fill the void, did not support the woman at home by helping her to alter the causes of her boredom and loneliness, but rather stated that she required freedom *from* home *for* "something else." The "something else" women's lib leaders advocated was a job outside home, which presumably would provide a woman with feelings of self-worth and accomplishment. This prescription was, and is, in accord with a prevailing social norm— the success ethic.

According to the success ethic, a man's function in life—his job, the title and paycheck that accompany it—determines his worth. A man is defined and defines himself by his job, which determines his position in the status hierarchy. Thus, the function of the man becomes the measure of the man.

Success-ethic conditioning begins in childhood with the question, "What are you going to be when you grow up?"; extends to high school, where a young man is classified into either a trade or degree program; and culminates with college, graduate programs, and professional schools that stamp him officially with a job, career, or professional label. From then on, a man is forever presented to himself and to the world through the stereotypes of the functions he performs in his work.

Because it's a job for which a man is programmed in life, the job becomes his reason for being. Personal development, personal relationships, are secondary to his career. "Achievement" takes top priority, and the success ethic equates achievement with money plus as much status as possible. Whatever personal sacrifices are necessary to justify that end must be made. Men no longer have jobs; jobs have men.

Now, jobs have women, too. Not only single women but married women with families. For women's liberation has become the latest spoke in the wheel of success-ethic mythology. The women's lib proposal that a job outside home would provide a woman with freedom from boredom and loneliness at home was a treatment based on the equation of the success ethic with freedom.

Men chained to specialization and sub-specialization, climbing the apocryphal ladder of success, seemed to lonely women looking out their picture windows, not enslaved, but free. Liberationists sought not to change the existing success system but merely to join it themselves. Their only quarrel with the success ethic was that it excluded women; thus, they sought to ameliorate the inequity by seeking for women the same kind of "freedom" they believed men enjoyed.

The woman who herself subscribed to the success ethic became an active liberationist. If Man could be fulfilling himself "doing important things in the world" she'd show him she could, too; so Woman fled home in imitation of Man. And the man of the day was the Hollow Man, the Computerized Man.

Never was Man less in need of emulation and more in need of searching his own soul. Never was he less free—and more enchained. But nonetheless, he was out There—out in the world, away from home—and Woman followed him; not to bring him back, but to compete with him there on his own shaky ground.

Ironically, at this pivot point in social history when families needed more than ever before to come closer together, women by the thousands began to flee home and families grew farther apart. For the notion that women would be liberated by jobs outside home was innovated and perpetuated by female devotees of the success ethic.

In theory, it appeared that a job outside home would solve the problems faced by the woman raising a family. In fact, for many women it compounds existing problems or creates new ones.

There is a vast discrepancy between feminist theory and the realities faced by working mothers. The discrepancy results from the great paradox of the women's movement—the fact that most women's liberation leaders are women without firsthand experience in making happy family lives—women who have been divorced, or who are unmarried—while many of their followers are women with husbands and children. Nonetheless, feminist theorists have maintained to their followers that a woman can combine a stimulating full-time career and a fulfilling family life; that she can have it both ways.

FEMINIST THEORY

Children are no reason to stay home, the theorists argue; the man is a parent, too, and he doesn't stay home with the children, so why should his wife? A woman can have a job outside home, but still have time with the family in the mornings before school, during the evenings, and on weekends. It's the quality of time that a mother spends with her family that counts, not the quantity, they insist.

And out of this mythology has risen the greatest phenomenon of the twentieth century—Superwoman!

Superwoman emerged fully grown from the minds of women who either didn't choose marriage and family or who are divorced; yet Superwoman has become a prototype for all women, including those with husbands and children. Theoretically, Superwoman has a challenging, creative career, through which she contributes to society; and in addition, she spends "quality" time at home with her family. Without the benefit of pep pills to enfuse her with artificial energy, or tranquilizers to calm her nerves and ulcers, she runs a beautifully managed ship. She's with the family until the sitter comes, the children are dropped off at day-care, or leave for school; then she's out the door herself for a full and creative day away from home.

Superwoman has unique employment opportunities. She has a "man's job" at a "man's pay," but unlike most men with "stimulating," "creative," "fulfilling" jobs like hers, she is not expected to bring work home with her. She leaves her work and decision-making responsibilities at the office, shuts off her worldly mind at 5:00 P.M., races through traffic, and is relaxed when she arrives home at 5:30 (the children have either let themselves in with keys earlier, been with a sitter, or been picked up from day-care). Superwoman converses with them, serves dinner, has a pleasant evening with the family at home, or attends a concert or movie with her husband. Superwoman doesn't let herself go to pieces or to pot; she manages to get in some exercise, read the latest books, and have a hobby or two.

Superwoman is free weekends to catch up on household management, grocery shopping, and cooking. (The theorists say that Superwoman's husband should help with these things, otherwise he's a masculine oppressor.) Thus, Superwoman and her family spend the weekend doing chores, which supposedly brings them closer together.

Because Superwoman's creators have no positive firsthand experience as wives and mothers and little real concept of the ongoing interpersonal relationships that are part of family life, they tack the family on as an addendum to a day at the office— an afterthought. That is their perception of combination career and marriage! Thus, Superwoman—who's patterned after Computerized Man—lives in the writings and imaginations of the theorists who created her.

WORKING MOTHER'S REALITY

According to many of the women who try merging careers outside home with raising families, life is not so free, fulfilling, and glorious as the theoreticians would lead one to believe. On the contrary, many women report that, instead of the hoped-for feelings of challenge and excitement, their dual roles bring feelings of frustration and tension, of being pulled in two directions. Working outside home creates new problems, without solving old ones.

The most frequent complaints of the woman who combines working outside home with raising a family are generalized feelings of overcommitment and dual loyalties; alienation from her family, boredom with her job, lack of time for personal self-development, and feeling that what she's gaining from her job is not creative fulfillment, but money.

"My profession has taken more out of me, and out of our family life, than it's been worth," says a woman attorney who's practiced in a large law firm for the past twelve years while raising her family. "I feel that by working I've sacrificed a closeness I might have shared with my three children, had I not been divided in my loyalties all these years." Another woman dissatisfied with the application of feminist theory to her own life says she is leaving a job she's held for two years as an educational psychologist because "I have come to realize that there is nothing I am doing in the world of work—or that I ever will do no matter how high I go—that can't be done by somebody else. But nobody else can do for my children what I can do."

A woman's feelings that family life suffers because of her job are often compounded by knowledge that the job itself robs her of time and opportunity for personal growth. A history professor and mother of two children, who has worked for the past ten years, says, "I'm frankly bored with what I'm doing professionally. It's become quite routine to me now that I've proven I can make it. I've come up through the promotion ranks, I've published in respected journals, but the price that I've paid in addition to lack of time with my family is the realization that while I've developed as a history professor, I've not developed as a person."

Lack of personal development is a frequent concern of the woman who has been working for ten, fifteen, or twenty years and who arrives at age forty or forty-five burned out. Bored. The children are fairly well grown; the job—regardless of how seemingly exciting—is routine. "Where am I going from here?" is the question asked by the woman who has merged a career with motherhood as often as by the woman who has not.

This is not surprising in view of the comparison group. How many men who climb the ladder seeking the American dream find it a nightmare? How many men who have "made it" in terms of status and money find themselves bored, looking for new meanings and challenges in life? Many of them, as is evidenced by the fact that more men every year are making mid-years career changes—chemists turning to business; businessmen returning to college to become teachers, lawyers, or scientists. It's hardly surprising, then, that women who have been working, and trying to make homes besides, have similarly concluded that work—even stimulating work—can be routine, and when it becomes routine, boring.

Many working women with families find after the first flush of success—of landing a job, of arranging for sitters or day-care, of juggling schedules—that in addition to the drain on their personal and family lives, there's nothing very creative or glamorous about working.

"I've come to grips with the fact that working neither enhances my relationships with my family nor gives me a feeling of personal fulfillment," says a school librarian who has worked for the past eight years while shuttling her two children between sitters and day-care centers. "I am working for the money. Even with child-care costs, my salary raises us from the $15,000 a year my husband earns to over $20,000. My job pays for the extras—the furniture, clothes, trips, that we otherwise couldn't have."

Regardless of the specific job, many women teachers, lawyers, social workers, psychologists, nurses, and professors express similar feelings. "I work for the money, otherwise I wouldn't be doing it," an architect and mother of two children, states flatly. "My husband's an engineer and he does well, but my additional salary has enabled us to buy and renovate an expensive home in a high-tax area. Our children go to private schools and camps; we go to Europe at least once a year. We'd have to cut back if I didn't work, and I don't know where we'd cut."

Clearly, a job outside home does not provide every woman raising a family with feelings of self-worth, accomplishment, or enjoyment. Realizing this, many intelligent, capable women do not choose to combine motherhood with a career outside home. Nor do they wish to be at home experiencing feelings of boredom and loneliness as did Friedan's women of the fifties and sixties. These women have found an alternative to either way of life.

1

The Woman Who
Chooses to Be at Home

This book is about women who have developed a life-style alternative called the human ethic. The ethic states that forming and maintaining close human relationships is at the core of what life is all about, and is therefore to be kept in primary focus. Women who choose this ethic elect to stay at home to raise their families rather than to work outside home, and find at home not boredom and loneliness but rather enjoyment, feelings of self-worth and accomplishment. How do they do it?

My interest in this question was first aroused in 1964 when my husband, young daughter, and I moved to Cambridge, Massachusetts, to a street which I'll call Corine Street, an enclave of young families most of whom were "nuclear transplants," or as the sociologists say, "high mobiles." My first discussions with women on the subject of the woman at home were rap sessions, though the term was yet to come into vogue, held in cramped apartments while babies napped and toddlers played. What aroused my curiosity about the women of Corine Street was that although women's lib was starting to boom, and women with children were leaving them in the care of others in order to leave home themselves, the women of Corine Street were not. Why? I wondered.

The reason was straightforward. The women of Corine Street were not trapped housewives; they did not desire to escape home, because they enjoyed being there. They found happiness and satisfaction at home. How?

One explanation of their success was that while the women on Corine Street reflected a variety of educational backgrounds and work experience, each of them felt raising her family to be her primary commitment. Each had thought through her decision to be at home; each knew what she was doing and why she was doing it.

Another reason women on Corine Street enjoyed being at home was that none of them regarded housekeeping as a major occupation or preoccupation. While each did what was necessary, she did not a speck of dust more. This allowed each woman to distinguish between housework—much of which was unimportant—and the care of her children, which was of prime importance to her. These women were not mere custodians but rather interacted with their children, for the mutual benefit of parent and child. Moreover, in allocating priorities which placed their family life first and housework at a minimum, it was possible for each of these women to retain existing interests or develop new ones while she was at home, raising her family.

In addition, Corine Street was located where the "action" was—in the midst of crowded Cambridge, an easy walk to museums, shops; near colleges and universities. A woman was not removed from the mainstream of thought and activity because she was at home, raising a family.

The women of Corine Street were not bored with themselves, with their families, or with their contemporaries. Nor did they have the chance to become lonely and feel alienated. The usual problems of isolation created by the mobile society were greatly diminished or absent, because Corine Street provided a strong support group. Although immediate family and extended family weren't present, family substitutes were abundant. When someone was sick, there was always someone else to take over; there was privacy when one wished it, companionship when one sought it.

The members of the group reinforced one another in that a major emphasis—in spite of limited budgets, crowded living conditions, and high-pressure work situations for husbands—

was placed on quality family life. Husbands were an integral part of family life, rather than peripheral to it.

When I helped to co-ordinate a Harvard newcomers' organization in 1965, I continued investigating the factors which contribute to a woman's enjoyment of being at home by comparing attitudes between women who were happy at home with those who were not. Most of the several hundred women from various parts of the country affiliated with the newcomers' program were raising families—some, like the women of Corine Street, enjoyed being at home; others were classic "trapped housewives." What made the difference? One sharp contrast was that the woman who enjoyed being at home used her ingenuity and creativity to retain existing interests or to develop new ones while at home, but the woman who was unhappy at home often could not function productively away from school or office without someone else to give her assignments and deadlines. It never occurred to her to find new ways to use her abilities, if being at home precluded her doing things in old ways. Nor did she develop new interests if old ones couldn't fit into her new routine.

Moreover, the woman happy at home did not consider herself a "housekeeper," while the discontented woman almost always cited housework as an overwhelming and prime complaint, feeling that "housekeeper" was her prime occupation.

The more I talked with women about what determined enjoyment and satisfaction, as opposed to boredom and loneliness, at home, the more apparent it became that the woman who enjoyed being at home had consciously decided to be there and had definite goals. In contrast, the woman dissatisfied at home was often unsure what she was doing there. Some of the dissatisfied women felt their positions were forced upon them by society; others felt their husbands wanted them at home; but rarely did the woman unhappy at home feel that being there was her decision. Along with the feeling that she was forced by conditions external to herself to be at home (or because of these feelings), the woman dissatisfied at home lacked a clear vision of what she hoped to accomplish in human terms, in everyday life with her family. While the woman who enjoyed being at home saw herself as a companion as well as a parent to her children, the woman who was unhappy there invariably considered herself primarily a caretaker.

Another important difference was that the woman who enjoyed being at home perceived that she had a strong support group—either in terms of a community of other persons with similar goals, or of other families who valued family life, or both. In contrast, the woman unhappy at home often felt stranded, living among strangers, or in areas where other women were also unhappy in their situations.

When the woman enjoyed being at home, her husband was continually involved in the ongoing life of the family; where the woman was most unhappy, her husband was not actively involved.

Interestingly, many of the women dissatisfied at home did not wish to leave home to take jobs, nor to remain home unhappily, but rather desired to alter factors at home. Such women wanted to raise their families themselves, but sought more effective ways of doing so, and also sought personal development simultaneously.

After returning to the Midwest in the late sixties, I served as a women's adviser, concentrating on the particular needs and concerns of the woman who elects to be at home to raise her family. My experience with the women with whom I've worked and with women from various parts of the country whom I've interviewed specifically for this book has borne out what seemed evident in the Harvard community: that the attitudes of the woman who enjoys being at home—and the ways in which she puts these attitudes into practice in her daily life— differentiate her both from the woman who stays at home but does not enjoy it and from the woman with children at home who chooses to work outside home.

Woman at Home focuses on those women who elect to be at home and who derive feelings of enjoyment, self-worth, and accomplishment from this option. The following chapters illustrate, through the personal experience of these women, ways in which a woman who elects to stay at home to raise her family can give the most to and get the most from this life-style decision.

2

Three Phases of Life

The woman raising a family can integrate her personal interests and activities into her total life scheme; she need not forego them or leave home in order to pursue them. Many married women with families find making a home and developing personal pursuits complementary, rather than conflicting, aspects of their lives. What is distinctive about the woman who achieves balance, without conflict, in her life, is that her question is not whether or not to take on activities in addition to raising a family, but rather when and where to do so.

There are three distinct, but contiguous, phases in her life, for which each woman raising children can plan. The first phase begins with the birth of the oldest child and lasts until the youngest child enters grade school. The second phase comprises the years when the children are in school. The third phase—which is a new-lease, rather than the empty-nest period —begins when the last child leaves home.

The first phase is the one which many women discover allows time for building a foundation for themselves as well as for their children; a time that they have found can be spent primarily at home, where they are with their children on a day-by-day basis, yet can also be involved in different kinds of activities if and when they so choose.

While some women become so involved in personal endeavors at home that they stay there after their last child is in grade school, others find the second phase a time to get involved in activities outside home—in the community, at college, through part-time jobs—which allow the flexibility of being at home after school when their children are there.

Some women become so interested in one or more of these endeavors that they go full-speed ahead once the last child leaves home, giving full time to their own schooling or to a job. Others go off in a brand-new direction.

Whichever ways a woman chooses of implementing these three phases one thing is certain: a woman need not sacrifice one aspect of herself for another. The two major freedoms in being at home are interdependent, rather than independent. One freedom is the opportunity to create a secure home for herself, her husband, and children, within this vast social order. The other is that while making a home a woman has the chance to develop and expand her own interests, creative potentials, or personal specialties right there.

PHASE ONE—WHEN THE CHILDREN ARE AT HOME ALL DAY

Realizing these freedoms, learning the art of combining them, is often difficult. Twenty-six-year-old Kathy Jacovi, a young woman who today enjoys being at home raising her two sons, utilizing the freedom of being there to develop a creative potential of her own, says, "Getting started wasn't easy. I suppose it was really like being new at anything. At first, I made a big job out of caring for the house, instead of realizing being at home with the boys was a chance to have fun," Kathy says. "I felt I had to be a good housewife every minute, so rather than playing outdoors with the kids, I'd be cooped inside cleaning house, and I'd putter around, cleaning some more, doing diapers, or whatever, while they napped."

Kathy's eyes filled with tears as she recalled, "I felt so lonesome, and really worthless, so much of the time. I was so miserable that by the time our second baby was born I felt like I was in a cage, literally withdrawn from the society at large, and afraid at the prospect of re-entry. I read a lot about women going to work and finding somebody else to take care of their kids. But I loved the kids, and I didn't want to leave them. It was just everything about being alone so much that got to me.

"Then," Kathy says, "I got to thinking about re-entering society and what it really meant. I guess what it meant was that I had withdrawn myself from the world around us because I thought society was downtown at the office. Then I began to see that the whole world wasn't at the office, and that, in fact, I was living in the midst of society as much as I was when I went to work everyday. I saw that the people at the grocery store were social beings, so were the mothers at the park, and the lady who worked in the bakery, and the old man on the second floor whose grandchildren and children lived in Florida, and the widow across the hall. All these people make up society and many of them were as lonely as I was.

"Once I realized that, I really began to see a whole new world at home, and I loosened up and started to form some relationships with those around me.

"I stopped and chatted with the neighbors in our apartment building and I was delighted at how friendly they were," Kathy says. "I started going out and walking with the children. I met other mothers, and began to make some friends, to feel part of the world again. And one rainy afternoon, while the boys were coloring, I sat down and colored with them. It was fun, and they were so exuberant about the sketches I did of them that the next day I got some charcoal and heavy paper and did some more. I kept drawing and sketching every day with them. My husband then began encouraging me to take an art course at the "Y" one night a week while he put the boys to bed. After that course I started in water colors, and now I'm working in oils."

Kathy and her husband had always planned on two children, "But now," she adds with a twinkle in her eye, "I've caught on to what raising a family is all about. I'm thinking about how nice it would be to have a little girl in the family."

When their family is complete and the children are all in school, Kathy wants to go back to college. "I had only two years before we were married, and I didn't have any idea of the kind of courses I really wanted to take. Now there's so much I want to learn, I could go forever. And I'll always keep sketching and painting. It's a wonderful creative outlet, a real medium of self-expression, for me."

Anne Raydon is another Phase One mother who has learned the art of enjoying her family, and who has used the freedom of being at home to develop both her administrative and her creative abilities.

Unlike Kathy Jacovi, Anne says that when her first child, Lisa, who is now ten, was a baby, she felt very free. "All of a sudden, I had no outside job, no schedule, no classes to attend. Nothing but a baby to take care of, an apartment to straighten up, and dinner to make.

"It was glorious to have time to think; I never had time before then, except when I was assigned to research a particular subject for a particular class." (Anne has a B.A. in English, an M.S. in biology, and worked as a laboratory supervisor until a few months before her first child was born.) "Being at home also gave me time to read. Not assignments, but anything and everything that I wanted to read. And I had time to watch Lisa grow on a minute-to-minute basis. Those days were wonderful!"

When her son was born two years later, Anne recalls, "I was substantially busier. For the first two years of Tommy's life, I hardly read a book. A new baby and his jealous sister, and then a toddler and his active colleague sister, were all I could cope with at the time. They took every minute and I sure had fun with them.

"Then, it seemed, when they were about four and two, they became a self-sufficient pair—so long as I was within earshot. I still played with them and took them places frequently, but they played together for long periods in the morning, and again in the late afternoon. I began reading again, and I started on a sewing kick. I'd never had any patience with home ec courses— too slow—but I dragged out an old machine of my mother's, bought remnants of inexpensive cotton, and began whipping up things for the kids and long dresses for myself. I even sewed a few things for friends. During that period, I was also in charge of a community ecology project."

When Lisa entered an experimental continuous-progress

school, Anne became heavily involved. "The school only succeeded because of the tremendous parental involvement and effort," she says. Anne taught a course in ecology one morning a week at the school, bringing Tommy along with her. "He loved his day at 'big school,'" Anne recalls. "And he felt right at home when he began going there himself."

When Tommy started school, Anne spent several mornings a week teaching and helping develop a new curriculum. Then she cut back when the new baby, Ro, joined the family.

"Being at home much of the day with only one preschooler is quite a change from the hectic times I had with two of them," Anne says. "Ro and I spend a lot of quiet time together, until Lisa and Tommy get home in the afternoon. Then, of course, it's all noise and commotion until bedtime."

Anne discovered an interest in photography during the two years she's been at home with Ro. "My husband got a new camera for his office. But it never made it there. I picked it up the first day it came, shot a whole roll of Ro in action, and have been hooked ever since. I've done a brochure of photos for our church and am also developing quite a folder of art photography. During the past months, my work has been exhibited at several local art shows."

Summing up her feelings on combining her other interests with raising her family, Anne says, "The secret of the whole thing is balance. Some years there's time for more of one kind of activity, less for another. There have been times, like when Lisa and Tommy were small, when I played with them all day, and I loved it. Then, other times, when I spent a great deal of time with them, yet did other things, alongside them, too—reading, sewing, ecology projects—and I've loved these periods, as well. I also enjoyed my heavy involvement in the school. Now, with Ro, I just take the camera along when we're out, she rides her trike, and I capture the world through my new lens."

PHASE TWO—WHEN THE CHILDREN ARE ALL IN SCHOOL

Marion Leberg, a woman busy with four school-age children, expresses feelings articulated by many other women when she says, "I believe there's a time and place for every aspect of one's self. My time is here and now for my family, and to a lesser extent for my other activities. In a few years, the children will all be grown and things will be reversed."

With her oldest son now a senior in high school, the youngest in fifth grade, Marion says she finds this period of growth and development "the most demanding years ever. When the children were little it was fun and games; my husband Paul and I always talked and played with them a lot. But now, we have four more adults in the household, plus loads of their friends, and the conversation zips constantly on all subjects. And through it all, it's evident that the kids don't pay nearly as much attention to our words as to our deeds.

"Paul and I feel raising our children to be compassionate, decent human beings is the hardest job we have," Marion says. "And when I say 'raising' I don't mean seeing them every so often to tell them a few things. I mean being right there, on the spot, doing what you believe you ought to be doing. It doesn't matter what you tell your children; they won't listen to what you say, but they'll watch what you do! That's why Paul and I have always operated on the premise that our lives are statements of our beliefs."

Marion lives what she believes, and she believes in "the total family unit coming before personal considerations of either husband or wife." Marion says, "I've always had a penchant for politics, and have been involved in the Democratic party since I was able to vote. When I was home with preschoolers, I kept my hand in politics in the most basic ways. I did whatever I could from home, including licking envelopes (the children helped), calling lists, and typing memos." Since Marion's children have all been in school, she has had the time for more active political involvement. "I go into headquarters during their school hours, at the height of hectic campaign times and otherwise work from home between elections."

As campaign manager, Marion was responsible for the landslide state senate victory of her friend and neighbor (a woman with grown children). Marion herself has steadily refused to run for office because of the time she feels it would take from her family.

"Then I'd be just another do-gooder out saving the world while who knows what goes on at home. This way, I feel I'm able to raise the children and enjoy it and still keep up on the political scene. There's a time for everything, and my time for another full-scale commitment isn't here yet. It will come later on, but right now I want to be on this scene after school and on weekends. The boys will all be grown soon enough—I'm not rushing it!"

PHASE THREE—A NEW LEASE

Women who enjoy Phases One and Two, who put a great deal of effort and energy into these periods, usually needn't worry about an empty nest. Because, women who build close relationships with their children rarely lose touch with them when they reach adulthood. Many women now in Phase Three have grown children living in the same city, often with children of their own. Others have children in other parts of the country, who stay in touch by phone, and visit back and forth regularly. The women themselves are frequently more active than ever. Some pursue an interest which they developed while raising their families; others try new areas.

Fifty-two-year-old Donna Phillips is a Phase Three woman who speaks enthusiastically both about her busy past and equally busy present. When Donna married soon out of college, her husband started his dental practice in a suburban area. Donna, who taught piano before they were married, says, "I kept at the piano an hour a day no matter what during the early years of our marriage. The children were born, three of them in five years, and I was busy, but not too busy to practice. I raised them at the piano bench."

When the third baby was toddling, Donna decided to teach piano at home, "but I did it slowly. I figured I could always add students, but dropping them would create hurt feelings on their part, keeping too many would overextend me."

So Donna began taking three students a week. "It was fun to

teach again. And, although I never charged much, those lessons enabled me to pay a high school girl to come in for two hours on lesson afternoons to help me. She played with the children during the half hour I taught, then she did the laundry, dusting, vacuuming, whatever the house needed most that day for the remainder of the time. It was just great because I stayed involved with my music and in the process freed myself from most of the housework. It's amazing what just an hour or an hour and a half a day of someone else's help did to boost my morale—as well as to clean the house!"

Donna taught one student a day until all three children were in school; then came a choice point. "I could have taken on more pupils after school, but that was the time our three children were home, so obviously that was out," she says. "I could have convinced the principal to release my pupils during school time for lessons (others had done so in the past so that there was a precedent).

"But then I started thinking that while my pupils could get out of school for their private lessons, there were children in the school who would never have the opportunity for lessons at all. So, I arranged to have a piano donated to the school, and I volunteered to give lessons there three mornings a week. The students who were without a piano to use at home were allowed to practice there after school.

"I did this all the years we lived there, and it worked out beautifully. You know, one of my students just came to see me recently. She started with me in the school basement, and as a teen-ager saved baby-sitting money to buy her own piano. She's just graduated from the university in music ed. I guess that's the most gratifying thing that could have happened."

Donna speaks enthusiastically about the years she spent in her suburban area, of her participation in the community, of her volunteering in the school, of the "good family fun we all had." Then came another "choice point." This time it was a whole-family decision.

When their first child was about to enter college, Donna and her husband Fred, who had built a busy and successful dental practice, did some very heavy evaluating. They would have all three children in college within the next six years—at least two of them at once. They lived almost an hour's drive from the state university, too far for the children to commute. This would mean dorms or rooming houses, seeing the children occasional weekends and holidays.

"Fred and I knew what we wanted to do—we decided to sell our rambler with its spacious yard and move to the city. We bought an old Victorian house near the campus, and the children lived at home during college. Fred gave up his suburban practice, but had no trouble getting started all over again in the city. He's an old-fashioned small-town dentist; he takes a personal interest in his patients and talks with them about their family and business problems as well as their dental problems. He cares. Within two years he was as busy here as he used to be there."

What did Donna do during this period of her life? "In effect, I ran a no-rent rooming house. Students were here day and night. We had the children's friends sleeping here, eating here, and sometimes living here. I cooked, I listened, I talked; I had opportunities to take a good teaching job in a music school, and of course, I could have taught in our home. But I was having too much fun. Then, when Janie, our youngest, was a senior in college, and the boys were off to service, I started something new. I went back to school myself."

Donna didn't return to music. "Piano is part of me but nowadays it's an avocation," she says. "What I'd learned raising our family plus what I'd experienced with these kids on campus made me want to go into counseling. I felt qualified in a way I simply wasn't thirty years ago. So I went into a graduate program in psychology."

After she received her master's degree, Donna took a job in a family counseling service. "The work," she says, "is rejuvenating. I'm so fresh compared to people who have been doing this twenty and thirty years. A lot of them have lost some optimism by now, many of them are just plain tired of it—but I'm raring to go!"

Pleased as she is with her new job, Donna is glad she didn't begin it years ago. "If I had done it any sooner," she told me,

"I wouldn't have brought to my work what I do now, and it would have robbed me of doing all the other things I did. Do I regret the past? Those years at home with the children? Teaching music? Going to school? I'd no more trade those years for now than I'd have traded my own childhood. But that doesn't mean I'm not happy now. I'm doing just what I want to be doing; with a full life behind me, I'm starting another!"

Kathy, Anne, Marion, and Donna are among the many women who have discovered that other interests need not interfere with raising a family and raising a family need not preclude other interests. Each of these women has found that personal relationships and personal growth can be simultaneous and complementary. Each established priorities for what she does and when she does it; thus each has achieved balance rather than conflict within herself and her home life.

3

Death of the "Housewife"

The trapped "housewife" is dead. In her place lives the woman who enjoys being at home raising her family, ofttimes pursuing an individual interest there.

Housework is no longer the frequently mentioned enemy of the woman at home that it was a few short years ago. For today, the woman who chooses to be home does so because she believes there's much of importance to be done at home; that her major challenges and responsibilities are in the area of human relationships and personal development, which have nothing whatsoever to do with caring for an inanimate object— the house!

Some women use their children's nap times or quiet play-times to develop an interest which they themselves enjoy, doing housework only when they've first done what they feel is more interesting and worthwhile. Other women hurry through household chores to get to something more interesting which awaits; still others hire some help in the house to free themselves for their families and for individual pursuits. These women exemplify the prevalent new attitude toward the house, which states that the woman who chooses to be at home for the purpose of raising her family need not pay the price of hours of housework to justify her being there.

The woman who has not yet adopted this new attitude, but who wishes to, must first change her perceptions about her role at home. The first thing she needs to do, to gain the freedom to enjoy her family and expand her life, is to free herself from the notion that home is the place they live and she works. If a woman perceives herself as the family servant, then not only will everyone else assume her to be so, but she will feel guilty about time she spends playing with her children, enjoying activities with her entire family, and pursuing her personal interests. She will instead expend a great deal of needless energy cleaning the house and harassing everybody else to keep it clean. Once a woman realizes that raising her children, helping to create a secure family life, and engaging in personal interests are more important than keeping up wood and concrete, she can recover from the notion that she works for the family; a harmonious unit cannot operate on that kind of divisive premise.

A family has to find a means of dividing and delegating household tasks so that home can, indeed, be a happy retreat for every member rather than a place of drudgery for some. A number of proposals have been set forth during the past few years for handling the distribution of household chores. Among them are: (1) the woman leaves home and goes out to work—presumably either someone is hired to clean the house and care for the children, or the husband helps with housework after both he and his wife come home from work; (2) the man works outside home, the woman stays home with the children, both husband and wife share the chores; (3) going "halvsies"—each parent works half time, each is home half time and does his/her share of the housework; (4) role reversal—jobwife goes out to work, househusband stays home.

In no case does any one of these alternatives really address the problem felt by the woman who desires to stay home, but who doesn't feel housework is the price she need pay to do it. For each of these alternatives serves either to take her both from the housework and her children, to place an unfair burden upon the man who works outside home, or both.

Examination of each of these currently popular theories will make clear that none of them answers the needs of the woman who truly wishes to stay home and raise her family without burdening either herself or her husband with housework.

WOMAN LEAVES HOME

The proposal for avoiding housework more frequently advocated by hard-core feminists calls for the woman to go out and get a job and either "hire a housekeeper to care for the kids and the house," or farm her children out days and share housework with her husband evenings and weekends.

This is a facile solution which women who value raising their families reject at once, for it equates children with the housework. Leaving the housework and the children to the housekeeper equates the inanimate object—the house—with the persons who really matter—the children.

Putting the children in day-care while both parents work, leaving housework for both parents, is just as bad, for that kind of liberation from the house means liberation from the joys of raising one's own children as well. The notion that both husband and wife come home after a full day's work to share housework—and care of the children—obviously means that very little attention be paid the children, day or night.

An unmarried "women's liberator" spoke recently of visiting a former college classmate—"the poor thing, at home with four kids and all that ironing. She so needs liberation from it all . . ." Actually, the young mother does need liberation—from the ironing, not from the children. And the speaker needs liberation from the notion that housework and child care are synonymous.

The important aspects of raising children have nothing to do with housework. Yet time and time again those who purport to free women from housework really tell how to get out of the house to avoid work there, thereby leaving the children as well. That's because someone who does not understand or value family life, either because she has never known it or is too far removed from it in her present-day life to remember, assumes that everything around home—children included—is dull, routine, and needs to be escaped.

The constant lumping together of housework and child care in thoughts and actions can be disastrous to both a woman and her family because the woman who is able to differentiate clearly between baby and bath water is usually far happier than the woman who confuses the two.

For the woman who wishes to be at home raising her family, leaving home is simply no answer to the problem of being buried under household tasks. The real solution is getting on top of the chores, of doing those things which she can do quickly and easily herself, and of finding other people to do what she chooses not to do.

HUSBAND DOES IT INSTEAD

A currently popular solution to the question of finding others to help is that the man work outside home, the woman stay at home caring for the children, and both parents share the chores. But while the man's doing it may seem a solution, it's nothing more than a temporary expedient and often causes more problems than it solves. For the man who must come home after a full day's work to vacuum and scrub floors will not come home for long!

It would seem only just that the woman who opts for the traditional division of labor—where her husband works outside home enabling her to be at home—be willing to manage the house. But managing the house need not mean doing all the housework herself.

"GOING HALVSIES" AND ROLE REVERSAL

Another proposed solution to the woman's doing housework is "going halvsies"; both parents work half time outside home, both share the chores. This is an unfeasible solution within the present structure of our economy, but there is a more fundamental reason that this alternative is not likely to succeed. For, when it comes right down to it, many intelligent, capable women don't want to trade the freedom of being at home, raising families, and pursuing their own interests there for the burdens of a full-time or even a part-time job outside home.

And that is why role reversal is unlikely to become the norm in our society. Unless, that is, the men's liberation groups which are forming in various parts of the country gain momentum. Unless the men organize nation-wide, kick and scream, expose the exploitation they've suffered for centuries, complain that they're mere meal tickets, that they're forced into myopic, highly specialized roles in the social order, never free to explore new interests, never given time to know themselves, let alone their families. If that happens, many women may find themselves out the door, forced into jobs outside home, victims of male consciousness-raising.

But, until this occurs, many women who have the choice will prefer to be at home, raising families; for with the world of home within the realm of choice, not duty, many women do not desire to throw it away. A woman who expresses this view particularly clearly is Paula Otter, who had a top-level administrative job before leaving it when her twins were born two years ago. How does she feel about running the home as opposed to running part of a large corporation, as she'd once done? "My husband and I are each confident we could be wearing the other's shoes, but neither of us chooses to. I know I can succeed in the working world outside home; he knows he could run our home and care for the children, so neither of us needs to prove anything to the other or to ourselves. As long as he's willing to bear the pressures of the outside work world, and support us, I'm delighted to manage the home front."

Paula has articulated what many women who choose to be home feel: that when the traditional division of responsibility is no longer imposed, but is a matter of choice, clearly women have a pretty good part of the deal.

What then is the solution for the woman who wants to be home with her children and who has other interests to pursue at home—housework not being one of them?

MANAGING THE HOUSE

A sensible way to look at household management for those families where the wife need not work outside home for economic reasons is this: if the man is willing to put his talents and energies into being the major breadwinner, then he should not have to come home and make the bread as well. If a woman is putting her talents and energies into raising the children, making a total family life, and developing her own resources as well, then she should not be expected to do all the household chores herself. But she can manage the household —there is a big difference.

Managing the house is different from making a home, and it is also different from doing the housework. There are a variety of options from which a woman can choose her management techniques; she can combine two or several of these options, or employ various alternatives at various stages of her family life.

Among her options are eliminating a number of household chores entirely because having anyone do them is unnecessary to the life of the family; teaming up or trading services with friends; doing part-time work at home to pay someone else to come in to do what housework she would rather not; and hiring someone to come in to help, paying them out of the joint family account.

EVALUATION

In order to select from her options and decide how most effectively to manage the house, a woman who doesn't like housework needs to evaluate which parts of the total housekeeping picture she really likes least. She may find that she totally detests dusting, vacuuming, and bed-changing; that she doesn't mind running loads of laundry; that she is willing to wash the kitchen floor for the exercise; and that she enjoys cooking.

Or, she may hate scrubbing floors and cooking and vacuuming, while she doesn't mind running a dust rag in the least. The point is there may well be parts of housekeeping she finds tolerable, if not likable, which don't interfere with her enjoyment of being at home with her children, or with her other interests.

Once she knows which parts of housekeeping she really dislikes and wants to be rid of forever, she can plan to eliminate them. There are others who will do these things for her willingly and cheerfully, in exchange for either her money or her services. Just as there are women who choose to do housework in their own homes because they either enjoy it or don't really mind it, there are also women who choose to work in the homes of others, not because they can't find any other kind of work, but because they find housework satisfying and much less sedentary than many other occupations.

Some women actively enjoy housework and say they find it rather relaxing. Others who don't care for most housework, don't actively dislike it enough to want to explore alternative arrangements. While they don't think it is much fun, it doesn't bother them sufficiently to motivate their finding ways to manage it, other than doing it themselves.

Mary L. is independently wealthy, yet she insists on caring for a large home by herself. She has a couple of college degrees, she's a talented musician, she's a woman of many interests and activities. She is also a woman who enjoys doing her own housework.

Kay Bennington is married to a corporation president, and herself works part time as a translator for visiting diplomats. The mother of two school-age children, she does all her own housework and arranges and gives parties for fifty or seventy-five, at home, without batting an eyelash. Why doesn't she hire some help?

"I really don't feel the need to," Kay says. "I rather enjoy housework and love preparing for parties. Cleaning just doesn't bother me enough to make other arrangements. I have a kind of routine, I guess. I clean for an hour every weekday morning, then that's it for both prevention and cure. That takes care of laundry, things like bedmaking and breakfast dishes, as well as vacuuming and dusting. I just do a room or two a day. The children are very good about keeping their things tidy, and they help a lot, too. It's no big problem."

Women like Mary and Kay need not serve as models for every woman. A woman who dislikes housework shouldn't berate herself; she's not a failure at home, she doesn't need to go out and find a job to prove she's good for something else instead. Spending time with her children is what counts—communicating and interacting with them—whether she's doing her thing with them or they're doing their things with her. In ten years, nobody will remember if the kitchen floor was clean or not, but they will remember if their mother had time to sit at the kitchen table and chat with them.

Once a woman establishes what her priorities are at home, once she's decided which parts of the housework she will do and which she will manage, she is set to make her own arrangements. Depending upon her personal interests and economic circumstances, she may decide to team up; trade services; find an intermediary; or plan for help in the family budget.

TEAMING UP

One way a woman can help herself solve the housework dilemma is to team up with a friend, divide the chores in both houses, and each do what she dislikes least/likes most in both places. When my husband Dick and I were newly married and living on a Texas army post, my next-door neighbor and I shared our housework this way. Toni had a penchant for cleaning Venetian blinds, and the army apartment was filled with aging blinds. She suggested that we team up, I'm sure, largely to give herself double the number of blinds to clean each week.

Except for her preoccupation with the blinds, Toni knew a lot of housekeeping short cuts to teach a new bride. We enjoyed each other's companionship, and cleaning became a social occasion, rather than a time to dread.

TRADING SERVICES

In Boston, my neighbor Anne (who enjoys housework, hates cooking) and I traded services. She cleaned for me a morning a week; in exchange I went to her house two afternoons a week to cook their dinner. Now clearly, I had the best part of that deal. Except that Anne, to this day, claims that she did. Cleaning came easily to her—"I just shift my mind into neutral and clean away," she used to laugh—but cooking to Anne was real work. Cooking to me is a creative pleasure—no work at all—

which just goes to show that one woman's dessert is another woman's poison.

Today, there are housework co-ops springing into existence where housework is done for hours rather than dollars. So instead of trading services with just one person, several persons can form a four-way effort, or team setup. This means each does whatever chores for others she dislikes least, while each of the others does the same for her.

FINDING AN INTERMEDIARY

A woman may select as an alternative to trading her services, doing some other kind of work at home, then incorporating an intermediary into the picture to help clean the house. For instance, Donna Phillips, whom I mentioned earlier, gave one piano lesson each of three afternoons a week in her own home; this enabled her to hire a neighborhood teen-ager to come and play with her children during the half hour she gave the lesson and to spend the following hour and a half cleaning for her. Donna charged two dollars for giving the lesson and paid that amount to the high school girl who helped her. In fact, the piano student became the intermediary—the money went directly from the student to the high-schooler who helped clean, barely touching the hand of Donna, who gave the lesson.

"I wouldn't have lived any other way," Donna says. "I was able to spend the day with my children without worrying about the housework and had the fun of teaching a bit besides."

In contrast, there are some women who earn money either away from or at home, hate and complain about housework, yet won't hire any help. (I don't mean women who are the major breadwinners of the household. I'm referring to those who are working for personal rather than for economic reasons.)

Martha Peterson does medical secretarial work in her own home a few hours a week (she types from tapes, does insurance forms, etc., for a doctor for whom she once worked full time). Martha claims to hate housework, says she is chronically bogged down by it, yet wouldn't consider spending anything she earns to pay for help. "My paycheck goes right on my back," she says. "I love pretty clothes and this work gives me a chance to buy more than I otherwise can."

While Martha may not like housework, she clearly doesn't dislike it enough to put her money where her mouth is!

HIRING HELP FROM THE FAMILY BUDGET

Another alternative for women who hate housework is planning for some household help in the family budget. Many husbands who are sole breadwinners in the family are happy to establish budget priorities with their wives in which a household helper—a student a few hours a week, a professional cleaning person a half or whole day a week—frees their wives (and nowadays themselves) from some of the chores.

Whenever the subject of hiring outside help from the family budget arises, a myriad of questions comes along with it. Am I entitled to help? Can we afford help? Will it spoil the children? How much help do I need? Where will I find someone to help me?

Am I Entitled to Hire Help?

Why not? If a woman doesn't care for housework, and if housework can be planned for in the family budget, why shouldn't she hire someone to help with it? No one does everything well.

The idea that household help is a rightful expectation of the very wealthy woman while every other woman must clean the house herself is not only outmoded, but if one examines the notion closely, there are some very interesting insights to be gained.

In many ways, middle- and upper-middle-class families have had no trouble taking on many of the accouterments once belonging only to the upper classes. None of us balks much at buying a house or a car, or a new dress before the old one tears to pieces. Given the chance to travel, we'll go. We don't say that trips and houses and clothes and cars are somehow something we're not entitled to; and if we can budget for these things we make no pretense of being unable to afford them.

Yet when it comes to hiring household help, we're self-conscious. Somehow we suddenly can't see ourselves having someone else working for us in our own homes. We can't fit ourselves to the image (the grand dame, the President's Lady, the Queen of England). The idea of having someone else "serve" us is at odds with our democratic ideologies.

Yet none of us is bothered by having the check-out girl at the grocery store "wait on us," or the "carry-out" boy take our bags to the car; none of us minds going to a restaurant and buying food someone else prepared for us and serves to us. None of us refuses to try on clothes brought into the store's fitting room by a salesperson. But often we can't carry that easy acceptance of the buying and trading of services into our own homes.

Why not? One reason is that we fear being thought of as elitists (the Constitution; *Gone with the Wind?*). If we have someone working in our homes, then we perceive ourselves in the role of slave driver, oppressor, taking advantage of those who help us.

Poppycock! The kind of person who yells at waiters and waitresses, finds fault with the check-out girl for going too slowly, at the "carry-out" boy for going too fast, might well be a kind of supremist who thinks she's better able to do anything than anyone else. Or she might just like to harass people. In that case, nobody will work for her—for long anyway—so she doesn't need to worry about household help at all.

But if a woman is grateful for living in a society where she can buy services as well as goods; if she realizes she can't excel at everything, nor does she wish to; if she can manage the budget to hire the services of someone to help in the house; and if she feels household help takes priority over something else money would be spent on—then she deserves that help. She deserves it just as much as any other honest service she buys with any honest dollar.

Can You Afford Help: Or Can You Afford Not to Have Help?

"How can we possibly afford help?" I asked my husband, a marketing and consumer behavior specialist, soon after he began his first job. "If we want it badly enough," he stated matter-of-factly, and then he cited some statistics to go along with the human observation we've all made: people frequently find they can afford what they consider essential.

Obviously, if a family is just barely getting by at subsistence level, with every cent allocated for minimal food, shelter, and clothing, household help is not a consideration available to them. However, many middle- and upper-middle-class families are potentially able to have some kind of household help if they establish it as a life-style priority and are willing to forego other things in order to pay for it.

Many families who say they can't afford help mean, rather, that they don't want it enough to forego something else. And that's fine, if the woman (or the couple, or the whole family) is satisfied to do the household tasks. But, if housework (or the woman's attitude toward it, or the combination of the actual work and her perception of it) causes trouble between the couple (she wants "liberation," "he's a masculine oppressor because he considers her a servant," "she's always behind, the house is always a mess," "she saves chores for me to do—she's at home all day, why doesn't she get them done?"), then getting some household help is much less radical than psychiatry, marriage counseling, divorce, or all three.

For some women, even a few hours a week of household help can make the difference between enjoying being at home and finding it a series of chores. Contrast, for example, Patti W., who stays home, martyrlike, and Joan L., who enjoys being at home. Patti complains that she is always doing chores, that she has no time for herself, that she cares about her family but has no time to enjoy them—and that she can't afford any help. Patti's husband works for the same company as her neighbor Joan's, and their salaries are about the same. Their houses are similar in size and price, and they each have three children. But their spending patterns and value systems are very different.

Patti's family has two cars; Joan's has one ("We never ride when we can walk," Joan says); Patti buys original oils and prints; Joan frames some of their favorite water colors and sketches done by their children; Patti has fine Danish furniture and expensive draperies—Joan's house is furnished in what she calls "early attic," a combination of furnishings discarded by friends and relatives. Patti sends her children to nursery schools and summer camps; Joan doesn't use nursery schools, and "we take camping vacations as a family." Patti maintains she "can't afford help." Yet she complains because she's constantly inundated by household chores, and trying to get out from under the diapers, vacuuming, and errands; she says she has no time for herself; she feels she spends too much time yelling at or about her children. Joan, on the other hand, relaxes with her family, attributes her feeling of well-being "in a large degree to the help I have a few hours a week. I didn't have any help for the first couple of years we lived here, and I was often 'down under.' Now, I really do feel 'on top'—a huge improvement, and well worth the relatively small cost."

Will Having Help Spoil the Children?

Some women fear that having household help might somehow give their children unrealistic beliefs about themselves; that the children might see themselves as little princesses and princes with servants at their feet.

This is true, of course, if their mother communicates an attitude that she is royalty who sits and watches her "maids" at work, breaking the silence only to shout commands. But if a woman genuinely feels the parents' helper is her right hand, and treats him or her with the same respect she treats everyone else who comes into her home, then her children will—as with everything else—take on her attitude.

Often it's in families where some help is hired that the children pitch in and help the most. This isn't so surprising as it may seem. It stands to reason that in a family where it's accepted that the mother does everything, she has never given responsibility to the children. However, in a home where the housework is organized and delegated—and some of it to someone outside the family—everyone within the family has his or her jobs, too.

"There are no servants at our house," says Claire S., who has a student help with cleaning and laundry two afternoons a week. "Our children know that. They are responsible for making their beds and keeping their rooms in order." Claire's children, ages nine, six, and five years old, have had, she says, "mealtime jobs since they could walk. They take turns setting and clearing the table, making some parts of many of our meals. They pick up after themselves and participate in family upkeep projects."

How Much Help Do I Need?

Once a woman starts paying to have someone help her, she usually finds there are many things in the house that suddenly don't need doing after all. In evaluating what needs to be done and what can be eliminated, a woman needs to ask herself: "If it isn't worth our money to have someone else do it, is it worth my time to do it myself?" In this way a woman can evaluate what actually needs to be done to keep the house clean and running, and what chores are throwbacks to the time when housework was thought to be a primary activity of the woman at home. Those time-expanding chores can, then, be eliminated.

The amount of help a family needs depends on what that family decides must be done in the house, and what is expendable; on the size of the house; on the ages of the children (older children can do much more to help than toddlers); and on what a woman plans to do in the house herself. Families usually find that when all housekeeping chores are evaluated and organized, those to be delegated to someone outside the family aren't terribly numerous. Six to eight hours a week, either one full day or two half days, seem to be about the average number of hours required by families who have additional help.

Whom Will You Get to Help You?

Once a family decides it will have help, there are a number of ways to find someone. College and university student employment offices and student newspapers are excellent sources; so are high school counselors, who are always glad to help students find part-time jobs. One can also use a regular employment agency, run an ad in a local paper, or post a notice in a nearby grocery store or shopping center. I've talked with women who have found capable helpers through each of these sources and I have used each myself at one time or another.

College students are wonderful parent's helpers because the student who applies to help in a home is usually the one who likes and misses his or her own family and wants to be around another family.

I've asked a number of students who have helped in homes how they feel about doing housework, and about whether they feel exploited. "It's like any other kind of job," Radcliffe sophomore Karen James once told me. "If you're well treated, feel needed, and as if what you're doing is important to the people for whom you're doing it, then it's a good way to get through school. If the people aren't pleasant to work for, then, like anything else, you look elsewhere."

Carla Meyers, a University of Minnesota senior, expressed similar sentiments. "I'd much rather help a mother clean house than work harder, longer hours as a waitress and get pinched from behind. That's the kind of job where I think a student is exploited. I'd rather work in a home anytime. Someday I'll probably be hiring a student to help me in my home. I think it's a good idea all around."

Many college students count on house and yardwork to earn their way through school. In fact, formalized student cleaning services are cropping up on many campuses from New York to Hawaii. Often the students come in teams—girls to do laundry, ironing, and light housework, boys to wash windows, do heavy scrubbing. But role reversal isn't surprising. The six-footer may run the dust cloth, the hundred-pound blonde may wield the mop.

I ran an ad recently for a male student to do yardwork and help clean out the garage and got a call from a wispy-voiced girl who asked, "Are you discriminating against women for this job?" I said I wasn't as long as the woman could work as hard and fast as a fellow could. She came, and she did!

Alice Johnson, who prides herself on being a professional cleaning woman, finds jobs through listings with an employment agency. She's in her mid-fifties and works three days weekly, each day for a different family.

When Alice hears talk about how hiring a woman to clean is "exploitive," she laughs. "I'm a liberated woman," she says. Two years ago she and her husband, who works as an upholsterer, took a six-week trip to Sweden and the Netherlands on the money she earned. Now they're saving for France. According to Alice, "I wouldn't take an office job for the world. I'd have to sit around and punch a time clock. I like to be active. If I worked in an office I couldn't take six-week vacations. Besides, I like seeing a home looking all nice and shiny and I like helping women who want their homes looking nice but who don't have what it takes to do it themselves."

Those who do have what it takes to keep a house in order, and who enjoy it, balance those who don't. Because of this, whether a woman finds a high school or college student who's happy to help in a home, or whether she finds an older person who is glad to help a busy mother, if she really wants to find someone to help, she can. A woman who is considering hiring household help should ask herself, "Do I want to buy the service of household help rather than some other service or goods?" If she decides that the answer is yes, she can evaluate exactly what she feels must be done in the house and seek someone with whom she feels comfortable and congenial to help do it.

Whether a woman manages the house by eliminating many would-have-been chores entirely, teaming up, trading services, finding an intermediary, planning for help in the family budget, or a combination of more than one of these arrangements, every woman at home needs to realize that she is not a wife to the house. Rather, she is a person with individual interests, a wife to her husband, a mother to her children, and a woman faced with the responsibility of guiding a new generation into the next millennium—with her heart and mind, not with her broom.

4

The Original Woman

Once a woman at home recognizes that "housewife" need not be a component of any of the three phases of her life, she is free to choose from a wide variety of personal options. At one phase she may choose to take on no structured activities—an option in itself—whereas at other phases she may elect to structure her interests.

A woman raising a family may choose—particularly during Phase One—to take on no other readily definable activities. The woman who makes this decision often feels pressure from two sides. Some persons ask why she doesn't do "something else" outside home; others ask why she doesn't do "something else" while at home.

The woman who achieves balance without conflict is the one who knows when to take on other structured activities at home and when not to do so. The what, when, and why of her "something else" is decided on the basis of her own priorities. In choosing to be at home, she has established certain standards for the quality of human relationships and kind of family life she wishes to develop. Meeting these standards means that her other activities and interests, the "something else" she does, have a different priority in her life, and often do not take ordinary forms.

There isn't a bright, able woman, with normally healthy children, who spends sixteen hours, seven days a week, concentrating exclusively on her family. (Radical feminists, in their quest for converts to the success ethic, frequently establish a "straw woman," whose identity is totally bounded by her husband, children, and the four walls of her house.) In reality, every woman does something else, at some times, while she is making a family.

Her "something else" often does not, however, bear a ready label. Because she selects non-structured activities, she does not fit into a prescribed niche in the social hierarchy. There is a difference between non-structured activity and non-activity. Non-activity means doing nothing, while non-structured activity refers to a huge range of activities which have no occupational labels.

The option of non-structure is open to the woman at home raising her family, but is out of the range of experience of most men and women working away from home. The chance to think, to read a book, take a walk, visit with an old friend, or make a new one, are among many non-structured activities which are unavailable to most persons except on weekends or vacations. Yet a woman at home, raising a family, has these opportunities on a daily basis.

However, when a woman who enjoys non-structured activities is asked what, in addition to raising her family, she does, she frequently answers that she is doing nothing she can easily describe. It is thus assumed that she means that she is doing nothing, since there is no niche in the external social order into which her activities—and her whole being—can be pegged.

Actually, what a woman almost always means when she says she isn't doing anything which is easily described is that she isn't doing anything which has a career-oriented label.

Some of the most intelligent, creative women are those who have no labels. One such woman is thirty-four-year-old Alicia Lewis, the mother of two children, who has had little formal education, reads most of the serious work that comes off the press, and critically evaluates all that she reads and hears. Alicia is a highly intelligent, self-educated woman, whose husband, a space scientist, says of her: "She keeps up for both of us. I can barely keep up in my field—things happen so rapidly now.

Luckily, Alicia puts me in touch with this world, and other worlds, too."

Ask Alicia what she does, and she shrugs, "Nothing, really."

Why does Alicia say she does nothing? "It's a kind of a brush-off, I guess," Alicia says. "A way of giving a nothing answer to a nothing question. You see, I feel when a person says, 'And what do you *do*?' instead of what do you think or feel, it's a very superficial question.

"You could make the argument, I suppose, that what I *do* is a reflection of what I think and feel, but that kind of *do* would be a broad composite of all my actions. The usual question, 'What do you do?' doesn't pertain to that—instead it's a quick, nothing kind of question—what's your occupation? So I give a quick, nothing kind of answer. What does that say about me? Absolutely nothing. So they shelve me into their 'nobody special' category."

Julie Yates, a sensitive young woman in her mid-twenties, feels a great deal of pressure from her peers to wear a clearly defined label. "And so," Julie says, "the most difficult part about adjusting to being at home with a child, I have found, is realizing that I have a perfect right to be here. I was doing graduate work in anthropology at UCLA when John and I were married. I stayed in grad school until Amy was born three years ago.

"I left school, and I'm not sorry, but because of my conditioning and the peer group pressure, both from women and men, I felt plenty guilty about staying home. I think my 'generation'—the under thirties—is really in a dilemma either way. We're raised with women's lib so we feel guilty if we don't go on to work or to grad school, then, out to work. But we also feel guilty if we leave our kids to do it. There is no chance, really, within the system, to stay at home and feel justified.

"So," Julie says, "I feel guilty about staying home with just one little girl, like I'm playing hooky. But I'm enjoying her so much, and I'm enjoying doing some of the things I didn't have time to do in school, like playing the violin, something I haven't done since high school. Not that I think I have any talent; in fact, I think I don't. But it's fun, anyway. Now, by the standards of my friends in school and at work, I'm 'doing nothing.' But I like it."

Twenty-nine-year-old Sue Wickersham expresses a similar view. "I haven't worked outside home for a day since we've been married," Sue says. "I feel so lucky to have this luxury of time. Clearly we could have more money if I worked; two salaries instead of one. But my husband is willing to have me stay home, and there is so much I enjoy here—I love being with the baby and I have a lot of hobbies. I garden, and we make almost all of our food—even catsup—from scratch.

"I'm very happy with my good luck, but the problem I find is in communicating the dignity of what I do to others. People like hearing a one-word or one-line description. The way it is I have to start a whole sermon when someone says, 'What do you do?' A one-word label would certainly be convenient, but," says Sue pensively, "sometimes labels can get you into a lot of trouble. I think that's been the problem with the hippie movement or civil rights. You know, you put a label on; it conjures up images in the other person's mind before they get to know you. In fact, I think a label really can prevent getting to know the other person—you tend to respond to the label instead of the person."

Bettye Jo Preston, a young woman busy at home with two preschoolers, and enjoying the freedom to "read, paint a little, have a little solitude," sums up both the problem inherent in explaining what she does, and her solution: "I used to get mad inside when somebody would say, 'And what do *you* do?' or 'What do you *do* all day?' I felt the implication was that I should be doing *something* and that being at home was construed to mean I was doing *nothing*. It was their tone or attitude more than what they'd say, I think.

"Well, I don't get mad any more. I just tell them what I do. I figure if someone needs a label to stick on me so they can say, 'She's an XYZ,' then it's their problem, not mine."

It is not only women with young families who frequently feel pressure from outside themselves to wear a label. Pauline Sherwood, a fifty-one-year-old woman who has two married daughters and a teen-age son, says, "There's a lot of talk these days about how a woman ought to go out to work once her family is grown, in order to be able to say 'I'm a something-or-other.' Many of my friends have done this, and if it's what they want, it's fine for them. But I don't feel the need. I like to read, to sew, to visit with friends, to spend time with my family, to relax in the evening with my husband. I suppose a job would give me a traditional kind of answer to the question, 'What are *you?*' when I'm asked. But I've got a pretty good answer for that. I just reply, 'I'm a human being, what are you?' "

Sue, Julie, Alicia, Bettye Jo, and Pauline have voiced what most women raising families have felt at one time or another: that one of the greatest problems of the woman at home is communicating her kind of freedom to others.

The reason it is difficult is that she doesn't fall into a readily describable category, or niche, common to the experience of the kind of person who asks, "And what do you do?" or "What are you?" Few persons, except other women who have had the good fortune to have a period of time at home doing "nothing structured," understand the meaning of the freedom of non-structure.

The way a woman can enjoy her freedom to care for her family, to enjoy non-structured activities of her own choosing, and not succumb to social pressure to do "something else" labelable is to develop a sense of pride in her individuality. Then, when someone asks her what she does, she can take their question for what it is—a simple question—rather than a demand for her to cram her whole being into a one-word label.

The woman who is motivated by her own interests, rather than by pressure from outside forces, to engage in structured activities in addition to her family life, can do so without leaving home to fill a niche in the workaday world. While many women realize this, others do not.

The success ethic assumes that the way to develop the self lies outside the self. Thus, the woman who desires to pursue other interests in addition to raising her family frequently goes out to an office where she fits herself into an already defined category, complete with a label, believing that in saying to herself and the world, "I'm a fashion co-ordinator," "I'm a secretary," or "I'm a lawyer" she somehow establishes her identity. Such a woman hasn't found a new identity, she's found a new mask.

Identity—the concept of self—is established from within. Feelings of self-worth, confidence in relationships with others, begin from the inside and radiate outward. The most secure, confident person is the one whose inner resources are firmly established in her own eyes. This kind of confidence projects itself outward.

The woman at home raising a family has, in addition to the chance to build strong personal ties with those closest to her, the opportunity to maintain her self-confidence by enhancing her concept of self in different ways at various phases in her life.

One of the most exciting options available to the woman at home is that of developing her own creative potential. Each individual is endowed with innate creative abilities, yet most persons are stifled by the success ethic before having the chance to explore or develop their existing potential. The executive who works a sixty-hour week has little or no time for his family, let alone for personal artistic development. Similarly, the woman who works outside home, in addition to raising a family, has little time or energy to explore her inner resources.

The woman at home does. Many women who have developed creative potentials they didn't know they had prior to being at home raising families are women who had little previous opportunity to participate in artistic endeavors. Particularly striking is the number of women formerly trained in the sciences—women with chemistry, physics, biology, nursing backgrounds—who had previously thought of themselves as without artistic abilities, until being at home gave them the opportunity to develop creative capabilities on their own.

Jane Mooring worked as a medical technician before her marriage, and has developed an avid interest in pottery-making since being at home with her family. She discovered the fun of creating "ex nihil," as she calls it, when a friend encouraged her to take a pottery course two months before her first baby was born. "I'd just quit working," Jane says, "and had some free time, so on a lark, I took the class with her. Funnily, my friend lost interest but I was hooked."

When her husband George saw her enthusiasm and enjoyment in the work she created in her classes, he bought her a potter's wheel as a Christmas gift. Jane houses the wheel in the basement family room adjacent to the children's play area.

"When George first gave it to me, I was thrilled, and also a bit afraid. It's an expensive piece of equipment. But he saw it as a basic investment, rather than a luxury. I have taken more pottery-making courses, and I have made us a set of dishes, as well as innumerable *objets d'art* and birthday and Christmas gifts for friends and relatives.

"But," Jane says, "the investment in the wheel has paid off many times over, not in terms of *what* I create, but in *that* I create."

Andrea Kingston expresses similar feelings about the music she composes. According to Andrea, who taught math and science in a private high school before her marriage, "Doing things at home on my own time schedule is exhilarating. For years I followed somebody else's formula, taught somebody else's thing. During college I was a research associate in a chem lab and essentially carried out somebody else's orders. Teaching was more creative, but I still never really felt I was doing things my own way. Chemistry can be highly creative if you're Madame Curie; if not, it can still be creative if you have your own project and your lab. Someday, perhaps, I'll go on for graduate work, but right now I'm busy raising our family and involved in a new-found creative outlet—composing.

"I never took music lessons," Andrea recalls, "I was always in a math-science track. About the only exposure I had to any formal musical training was in grade school when the singing teacher came, and music replaced penmanship class once a week." Andrea says her husband took piano lessons as a child "and when his folks moved from their home to a small apartment," she adds, "they gave us the piano which they felt we might want for our children."

For the first couple of years, Andrea never touched the piano except to dust the keyboard. "But, one day," she remembers, "I was humming a tune, while dusting, and something made me sit down and try it on the piano. I didn't know the keyboard at the time, so it was hard to make it come out, but I finally made it sound like it sounded when I hummed it. It wasn't a familiar tune, yet it didn't occur to me at the time that I'd made it up, either. I just felt driven to make it come out of the keyboard.

"After that, when other tunes came to me, I tried them, too. My husband taught me the basics—where middle C is, and a few chords. Later, I decided to take some lessons."

Andrea was afraid a "traditional kind of play-by-note-and-rote course would kill my creative instincts," so she found a teacher who would give her beginning lessons in music theory and composition. "My goal is not to be a great pianist, nor even a good one. It's composing that's such a fantastic challenge to me.

"I improvise a piece whenever it's all there, in my head. When the children are playing with each other or with friends, I sit at the piano and work it over and over. I fill pages and pages of the composition book until it sounds just right. I have constant delusions of becoming a female Beethoven, or maybe another Jerome Kern, while I'm doing this. But, my real enjoyment is the exhilaration I feel from doing something which is a constant challenge to me."

Mary Dawyers is a woman who, though she had not written before she was at home raising a family, has found writing to be a gratifying form of self-expression.

"I've been writing poetry for several years," Mary says, "though I never thought, before I started, that I had it in me. I think every one of us has a measure of creativity. It's just that a lot of people never have the chance to develop it.

"Being at home has given me that opportunity. In the first years, when the children were little, I used to sew and then embroider very delicate handwork on the blouses and bodices of the things I made. But since I began writing poetry, I've lost interest in sewing and embroidering altogether. It makes me think my measure of creativity is *finite*, and I prefer to apply it toward my poetry!"

Mary and five other women whom she met in a creative writing course two years ago "have just compiled some of our favorite poems, and with the help of an inexpensive insta-print process we have made a small book. We made no attempt to find an established publisher—none of us has published outside local papers as yet. But we felt ready for another step, and we thought this little book would give our work some exposure. We have placed the book in some local bookstores on consignment and it's going surprisingly well."

Mary, a language and art major in college, had "a couple of scut jobs before the children were born—one in a library, one with an insurance company. Nothing I'd ever want to go back to. I've always been intrigued with the development of ideas, and poetry writing gives me the means of developing an idea and executing it."

Mary Dawyers is among many women who have discovered that one of the most precious attributes of the arts is that they defy the degree mill. Undeniably, art courses are a means by which one may develop new perceptions and may learn a great deal about the use of color and line. Through writing courses, one may improve organization and construction and get practice in bringing ideas to the surface. But, whereas a person can go through law school, earn a degree, and become a "lawyer," no art program can make one an "artist," nor can a writing program make one a "writer." These disciplines are primarily self-taught.

Thus, the arts are a natural area of development for the woman at home raising a family who may not have a formal education. Sarah Turner says being at home with her children has allowed her time to "paint for sheer enjoyment. I began by using the kids' dime-store water colors, and worked my way to acrylics. I've taught myself by trial and error, and now and then take an art class from local artists who give courses near here in the summertime. Basically, I paint what I want, when I want. My husband has hung a painting I did for him for his birthday in his office, and we have a couple of my other paintings hanging in the family room." Sarah had always intended to go to college someday, but now doubts that she will. "I'm presently happy at home with the children and I realize that when they go to school I'll be able to devote a great many more hours per day to my art."

Carrie Nyman has had little formalized schooling but she has found creative writing as her medium of expression. "I dropped out of college after the first semester. I couldn't stand constantly being told what to take. I was always sitting in the library lost in a book, and I didn't want to have to stop reading something really good when the clock indicated it was time to go take a class I wasn't interested in.

"Besides reading, what I always did like was writing, and after I married and our children were born, I began writing at home." Carrie, who has published both poetry and short stories, says, "I write loads more than gets published. But, every once in a while something does, and that makes me realize that eventually more will. My writing has improved tremendously with practice, and I'm thinking of starting a longer work sometime soon.

"I love the independence of this way of life. I figure I have the best of both worlds—a family, and a form of creativity which I enjoy—and I didn't need a diploma for either."

The opportunity to explore creative activities while at home raising a family is open to every woman. There's no such thing as an "uncreative individual"—only a culturally conditioned one. Our society programs persons to follow somebody else's formula, to do somebody else's thing, to fill an existing niche rather than to create a new one. Once a woman breaks the cycle of this cultural conditioning, she is free for a whole new kind of exploration of self.

When (either through trying many forms of creative expression, or by happening on one) she finds a creative medium, a woman has another challenge—to use it wisely. For as long as she is in control of her activity rather than letting it take control of her, she's in no danger of becoming another kind of superwoman. She will not become so absorbed in what she does that it takes her from her family; she will instead moderate her activity so that it serves her, rather than allowing herself to become subservient to it.

A woman raising a family, and engaging in an artistic activity as well, has—in success-ethic terms—a hobby, or an "outlet." There is a thin green line between a "hobby," which has no label, and a profession, which has one. That line is called a dollar.

Often, a woman with a hobby or "outlet" begins selling that which she creates as a means of gaining exposure for her work. Selling is not difficult. There are scores of ways to gain exposure for every artistic outlet.

Many stores offer arts and crafts items on consignment. What's hardest is to muster the courage to show one's work. Once a woman is over that hurdle, she can find someone to display and sell it for her. When a woman has a set of paintings or photos she feels ready to show, she can have a friend send out invitations to a "showing" in her friend's home. Somebody almost always buys, if for no other reason than to say they did. Thousands of newspapers and magazines publish stories and articles on all subjects. If a woman polishes what she writes and persists in shipping it around, somebody will eventually publish her work.

The woman who has gone beyond the success ethic realizes that selling her work is not the real challenge—it's how she views selling that is. For while it is gratifying to have tangible proof that someone else thinks she has done a good job, selling puts a woman into a new frame of reference. Whereas previously, she may have been able to disregard the success ethic, once she's selling, she's confronted directly by the challenge to avoid becoming part of the system. A woman can avoid the success-ethic system by retaining the interest and motivations which led to the original "outlet" without her "outlet" becoming a chore. For example, if a woman paints purely as an outlet, she may enjoy it tremendously, as a creative means of self-expression. When someone first asks to buy one of her paintings, she may be thrilled. When someone first asks her to paint something measuring sixteen by twenty-two, yellow and orange to match their living room décor, she may oblige. If she likes doing it, fine; then she's still enjoying her outlet, and selling it besides. But, if she doesn't enjoy it, and feels it's a chore to do her own thing to somebody else's specifications, she's selling out.

A woman may paint two or three canvases a year that meet her own standards of excellence and give her great satisfaction. If she starts turning out a half-dozen a year to meet demand, she may satisfy her clientele, but lose the fun of creating what she wishes, when she wishes. She may also find that—rather than serving her as an "outlet" and as an additional challenge while raising her family—her painting interferes with her family life, and her family interferes with her painting. She will then feel overstretched, overcommitted, resentful, enjoying neither her art nor her family to the fullest. In effect, she becomes a superwoman in scant disguise.

This will not happen if a woman is aware of the potential hazard and seeks to prevent it. Women who enjoy creative activities at home—some who sell their work, some who do not—make clear that there are two ways for a woman to prevent the superwoman syndrome from interfering with creative satisfaction and family life. One is to use her own timetable; the other is to employ her own quality control.

If a woman begins, while she has preschoolers at home, to spend a few hours a week on a hobby, and suddenly finds that she's selling that which she creates, and that she could sell three times as much if she spent three times as much time, the secret is to wait. When her preschoolers are in school, she'll have the extra hours with no conflict between her family and her own thing. If she tries tripling her creative efforts before that time, not only will it detract from the years with her family which do not wait, but the conflict can devastate the pleasure she derives from doing her own thing. Once the fun is gone, she's just another cog in the wheel of the success system.

Every artist who has a family to support dreams of financial independence so he can have the freedom to create to his own specifications; freedom from pressure to sell too much, or too soon. A woman at home, raising a family, has that precious independence. She has the chance to develop and moderate her creative ability so that it works for her. She does not have to work for it. She is free to sell it, or not, without selling out.

When a woman first begins a creative endeavor—whether

painting, writing, sculpting, photography—it's natural for her to feel inhibited about having anyone else see her work. Then, gradually, as she gains confidence in what she's doing, she takes pride in her product and wants others to share and respond to it. When the chance to sell something she's created first comes, it's understandably thrilling. After all, we're conditioned to believe that if there's a dollar sign on it, it must be good.

When the novelty of selling wears off, which it quickly does, the artist who must sell to eat has to keep selling, while the woman fortunate enough to enjoy her art first and foremost for its own sake can decide when to sell and to whom. Anyone can sell her goods or her services, if the price is low enough. (That doesn't pertain only to the dollar value assigned one's work, but to the standards set by those who buy it.) If a woman has a creative activity which she enjoys, the greatest personal satisfactions connected with it are in the creation and execution of that which she has designed. Other personal satisfaction comes from the response of those persons whose knowledge and critical ability she respects. Selling comes to have value only where one has high regard for the standards of the purchaser.

The woman who has the luxury of creating independently of the price of her product often most enjoys the creative process.

Rita Pauling is one such woman. Rita, who worked as a sportswear buyer in a small clothing store before her marriage, then stayed home to raise her family, says, "I started playing with clay when my children did. Except they quickly turned to other things, while I molded apples and oranges, then small figurines. I became really absorbed. Sometimes I'd put the children to sleep, sit down and play with some clay, and two hours would pass like a minute." Rita gradually switched to different kinds of clay, next she set up a workshop in her basement, then she began having her work fired.

Friends admired her things and coveted the Christmas and birthday gifts of her own making. And friends of her friends began seeing the graceful figures and expressive faces she molded and inquiring where they could be purchased. Rita now sells her work, but won't work on orders. "I don't want to have to make a certain thing more than once. But I do send cards out to those who have indicated an interest in my work, once a year. I let them call for appointments to come and look—usually they bring people along and somebody always buys."

Rita isn't very concerned about whether they buy or not—that's probably one reason they do—what she does enjoy is the sculpting. She's found a special niche and has a confident attitude and approach to her creations. "I do what I feel—I want to make what I see in my mind come out of the clay; if someone likes what they see, naturally I'm pleased. But face it, I won't sell any of my very favorite things anyway. I'm the real judge of what I think is good work."

Rita began working in a creative medium, brand-new to her, when she was at home with preschoolers. What began purely as an "outlet" during that phase of her life became a great deal more to her when her children were all in school.

Similarly, many Phase Two women now enjoying artistic interests began to develop their creative potential at home, after their children were born. In such cases, the interest became a bridge between Phase One, where the woman fit "her thing" into nap times, or catch-as-catch-can while children were occupied, and Phase Two, where she had substantial time to devote to it.

One woman whose interest has grown with her is thirty-two-year-old Carol Bradford, who says, "I took advantage of the time my children were small to try activities which were new to me, things I didn't have time to do as a chem major in college. Among the new things that caught my fancy was jewelry design. I don't know why; I rarely wear jewelry myself, but I thought it would be fun to try making some. So I got some inexpensive beads and glue from a hobby shop and tried my hand. Then the kids and I started collecting pretty rocks in the summertime, and scavenged for colorful old bits of colored glass which made for some really unusual pieces of jewelry. After I got seriously involved, I took a night-school craft course in jewelry making, which taught me a few professional tricks.

"I did most of my designing when the children were napping or playing with their friends, sometimes an hour a day, never much more. Nonetheless, by the time they were in school, I'd accumulated quite a collection. One day, I showed some of my designs to the owner of a small boutique in our neighborhood.

She asked me to bring some of the medallions and earrings in on consignment, and they became quite popular."

Since she first began selling her work three years ago, several additional shops display Carol's designs. "I've had opportunities to take orders for my jewelry, but I don't enjoy working that way. The stores buy finished products from me, they don't specify certain kinds of designs in advance. If they did, I'd be turning out batches of the same design and it would get dull. This way, every one of my designs is an original."

Rita and Carol have each found a way to gain exposure for their work, and to sell it, without selling out. Each has done this by controlling the amount she does—both in terms of the quantity she produces and the quality of her work.

Mora Reis also controls what she does and when she does it. Mora, who has her R.N. and formerly worked in a hospital, says, "The last thing I ever thought of doing was writing." Nonetheless, since she's been home raising a family, Mora has published a number of free-lance magazine and newspaper articles and now is finishing her first novel. "Being at home with small children has provided me with the chance to sit down and write about some of those things which I've thought a lot about. If I had been working, even a couple night shifts, or a day or two a week, I doubt that I'd ever have had the time or the motivation to write a word."

Mora got started writing by submitting an essay to the Open Forum page of her local newpaper. "That first essay actually gave me my start. From that time, almost five years ago, I've written occasional articles for our paper, and in addition free-lanced other articles. I've been published in some good magazines, which has given me the confidence to write more.

"I began the novel," Mora explains, "which is a kind of exposé based on my experiences working in a drug abuse center, when I was up for night feedings with our third child. I couldn't go back to sleep at night; so I'd write from maybe three until five, then go back to sleep and feel so much better.

"I still don't write on schedule, but largely when I can find the time and feel the urge. I average an hour a day, most days, I'd say. I keep the typewriter out, and work a little during nap time, maybe twenty minutes after Phil and the older kids are off in the morning.

"When the kids are all in school I expect to devote a great deal more time to writing," says Mora, whose three children range in age from two to ten years. "Right now, I'm delighted to know I can do it, and I'll concentrate on keeping the quality as high as I can without trying to get too prolific. Later on, I'll write more."

Anne Raydon also developed a special kind of creative activity right at home. "I always considered myself an efficient organizer, but never an artistic person," Anne says. That concept of herself has changed, however, since Anne first experimented with a camera two years ago, and discovered through taking photos of her own children a special knack for doing "candid portraits." After seeing her work, several neighbors asked her to do portraits of their children, "not the staid, static, now-smile-and-say-cheese kind, but dynamic portraits which really capture the personality of the child. Their excitement over the results has led to calls from some of their friends.

"I only take one project at a time," Anne explains. "My family is my primary commitment and I don't want my photography to compete with it. I want it to remain what it started out to be—fun. Also, I have my own darkroom and have learned to do all my own developing. If I get too busy, I'll wind up sending pictures out for commercial developing and lose the chance to put many of my own touches on a picture. You know, I think that is what being at home has done for me— allowed me to put my own touches on in life. This extends to family life, my relationships with my husband and each of the children, to community work I've done, and still do, and now to my photography. It's enabled me to be an independent."

Every woman at home is, in a very real sense, an independent. Each makes her own special niche, through experimentation and exploration, with nobody telling her what to do or when to do it. And every woman at home with a family has at some point —though by no means at all stages of her family's life—the chance to discover and develop her creative potential should she so choose.

5

The Specialist as a Woman at Home

The woman making a family who is trained as a specialist in a particular field, be it medicine, law, natural or social science, business, or one of hundreds of other areas, may elect to "bank" her specialty while raising her family. The woman who so chooses usually does so with the sense of confidence that if she wants to use her specialty later, she can. There are, however, women who feel motivated, for a variety of reasons, to utilize a specialty while they are raising families. Frequently, such a woman is beset with conflict.

Conditioned to think her specialty must be used in certain preset ways, she believes she must leave her children with sitters or in day-care while she leaves home to do her thing. But actually, an increasing number of women keep their specialties alive while at home raising their families. These are women who have gone beyond the success ethic to redirect their specialties to work for them.

A specialty is an interest that's grown. And often it's an interest that gets funneled into a neat, already established set of qualifications, which takes one through a prescribed number of years of training or schooling, culminating with a piece of paper which says one is licensed to *use* his or her interest in a particular way.

Such licenses are beneficial, to an extent. After all, it's reassuring to know one's surgeon has gone through medical school.

However, our culture has come to deify specialization to the exclusion of remembering the kinds of qualities we'd hoped to find in the person behind the specialty. In fact, we've come to forget that a specialist is a person, and conversely many a specialist has come to forget we're people (teachers who don't seem to realize they are dealing with subjects not objects, physicists who develop a bomb for the sake of science, forgetting that science was once a product of humanity). Too often the specialist becomes a machine which functions independently of the implications of its actions.

A woman pursuing a specialty at home need not function like a machine. If a woman is trained in a special area, she can retain that *interest* that led to a specialty—the special qualities about "it" and "her" which merged—without her becoming a mechanized slave to it. She can use an existing specialty, or develop a new one, with the perspective that a specialty is one aspect of herself, not the exclusive definition of herself. A specialty is an interest which one chooses to use in a particular way. Anyone can acquire any number of specialties—learn the craft, or go to school, take the test, get the piece of paper; it's what one does from there that counts.

Whereas in the world of work a woman may have been limited to one particular kind of function in which she specializes, at home there are many paths she may take.

There, she is free to develop an appreciation of her specialty as a tool to open new doors and areas of knowledge rather than as an end (namely a means to earn a living or gain status) in itself. She can direct her specialty to work for her in a variety of ways; and the ways she chooses can correspond to the amount of time she has to give to her specialty at a given point in her life. When her children are small she might redirect her specialty by teaching it on a limited basis, either as a volunteer or for pay, or by designing a part-time job for herself which can be done at home. This job may be for someone else, but on her own time, or it may be strictly a self-generated job. Then when her children are older she might decide to take what she's developed inside her home outside, at her own pace—so she doesn't become overburdened. Later, when the children are no longer at home, she may feel she can spend much more time on her specialty either away from home, or at home—or, she can bank it and try something completely new.

Vera Meyers, who has an M.D., has kept up with her specialty, and used it throughout her married life, without having to leave her three children to do so. "My primary interest has always been to help others; medicine is one of my means," Vera says.

When Vera was at home with her first child, she realized that though she was living in a middle-class neighborhood, among college-educated couples, very few of the women around her knew anything about preventive medicine. So she set up an informal program in her home for other mothers. "I wanted to show mothers what good preventive medicine is—to help them learn ways to prevent their children from getting ill, help them recognize symptoms when the children *were* ill, and help them know what to check on at home between visits to their pediatricians.

"These days, with a great many pediatricians practicing by telephone, and women living away from their own mothers, who have 'been through it before,' a mother has to learn how, in a very real sense, to be her child's own doctor. I enjoyed helping my peers—both my medical peers (because in the long run it certainly helped the pediatricians)—and my 'other-mother' peers.

"But when my children all were in school, I realized what I was doing in our neighborhhood would be even more helpful to financially disadvantaged mothers." Vera then decided to set up an educational program in a center-city slum area.

Vera paced herself so that she taught mothers in her own home when she had preschoolers, went out into the center city when her children were in grade school, and ultimately became a public health co-ordinator for her state when her children were in college and she was past fifty. But, even at that, she designed the job specifications, picked her own staff, and chose her own working hours.

"I feel," Vera says, "that instead of grinding away for twenty years to 'get there,' I chose to develop a special way to use my specialty during the years my children were home so I could put being with them first." In the process, Vera Meyers became a one-of-a-kind person in a form of preventive medicine which she helped develop.

Kate Bradley has an interest in science and wanted to keep that interest alive while she remained home to raise her children. Trained in biophysics, Kate says, "At first I was sure that there was nothing I could do at home. I thought I'd be sunk without a lab. But then I started reasoning that it was silly to let my training go to waste. I was busy with the children but not *that* busy—they napped, they played with other kids, there was evening time when they were sleeping and my husband and I would read. So there was time to do something in my field—but how?

"I figured I had the will, I'd make a way," Kate recalls. "So I started sending out letters to professors at various universities explaining my situation, including my resumé, and asking if they had some part-time work abstracting from the scientific journals available. I knew that most people working full time in medicine and the physical sciences don't have enough hours to keep up in the literature in their fields. New material is being generated and reported all over the world at a tremendously fast pace; persons working full time in the field usually can barely keep up with what they're doing themselves let alone keep abreast of what everyone else is doing.

"I thought that as a trained scientist I could be of service to one of my colleagues, who working full time couldn't keep up on, let alone get ahead of, what's going on in specific and related areas. I sent out about ten letters and got three replies, from professors interested in having me do some work. I decided on the two from the university nearest to where we live.

"I abstracted literature for these professors for a couple of years," Kate says, "then wound up editing journal articles for them, and by the time the children were in high school found myself with a part-time university appointment co-authoring articles with one of them. When my children start college, I'll be ready to do my own research, having sacrificed no time with the family."

Thirty-eight-year-old Marge Lafferty has also found a way to use her special talents in a unique manner. "I sewed my way through two years of college in spite of taking full course loads and a slug of extra-curricular activities. After I was married, I didn't see why having a baby should prevent my sewing a little." Now, five babies later, Marge is still sewing—a lot.

Her sewing space is four feet by three feet, a converted closet off her living room, and she specializes in designing and fashioning evening and hostess gowns. "I sewed for myself when I was in grade school. In high school I made clothes for all my friends, just for the fun of it. I was never paid for sewing until college when friends of my friends started asking me to sew for them. Then, I started making evening wear, and now—aside from sewing for the family—'after five' clothes are all I do.

"I only take one out of every four or five calls that I get. The thing is, I get a bang out of designing these gowns; it's my outlet for whatever little bit of artistic ability I have. But I simply don't want to make a business of my pleasure. I am often asked, by other women who sew, if they can work for me. But my answer is 'no,' because I don't want the pressure of expanding. I always encourage them to start themselves, though. I think more women would do this—sew right in their homes—but they don't know how to get started. The way to begin, I always say, is 'just spread the word to your friends; they'll tell everyone else.'

"My only problem is keeping the load down, so that I'm only doing one dress at a time. I have a whole family to spend my time with, and I take a class in the extension division of the university near us every semester. I'm going to get my B.A. one of these days, but I'm glad I didn't finish school ten years ago. Then I might have gotten smug and said, 'Well, I know it all now.' This way, I'm constantly learning, in the classroom and also from the incredibly sharp minds of the students around me. I don't feel that I'll ever stagnate if I keep on going to school."

Marge figures she spends two or three hours a day sewing. "Yet, the beauty of it all is that sewing never seems like work

to me. I'm doing something I really enjoy, that's the glory of it
—the fact that I get paid besides seems almost incidental.

"I save the handwork to do when I'm sitting around with
the family at night. I always do it plunk in the center of the living room so I'm right there seeing what's going on. I do the
cutting and machine-sewing in the late morning and early afternoon when there are only two kids at home. They're with me
when I sew; I'm sewing right by them when they're playing.

"People always say, 'How do you do it with five children?'
but I didn't have them all at once. I've learned over the years
how to budget my time, to do all I *should* do and all I *want* to
do. I don't have a set schedule or anything, but I have a feel for
what I can do, and I do it—no more."

Laura Evanson also discovered a way to use her specialty in
an unusual manner. Laura trained as a speech pathologist and
wanted to pursue her interest in helping children with speech
problems, as well as to research the origins of some of the im-
pediments. Yet as the mother of three preschoolers, she was
loathe to work outside her home. So Laura converted a small
den off the family living room in her suburban home into an
office and began tutoring students there. She had two students
a day, three days a week. Her income enabled her to hire a man
to clean for her once a week, and to have a high school student
come in and play with her own children while she tutored.

"I was always relaxed because I was right in the next room if
anything went wrong with one of my kids," Laura says. "They
knew where I was, and I knew where they were. I actually tutored only six hours a week, yet it rounded out my life wonder-
fully for me." When Laura's three children were in school she
wrote up the results of the methods she'd used during the time
she tutored at home. She had kept careful histories on her students, including detailed data derived from interviews with
their parents, and came up with some unique answers to the
complex questions of origins of speech problems. Her study was
published and led her to starting a training program for speech
pathologists to do essentially what she did; to work with children in homes (either their own homes or the teacher's home)
away from the school environment. She gives these courses,

three mornings a week, leaving her free when her children come home from school.

Laura knew her own priorities and, therefore, wouldn't consider leaving her children to pursue her own interests. In choosing to stay home she didn't then sulk that the world was going on without her; she simply figured out a way to bring a part of the world to *her*.

Callie Westberg began utilizing her specialty at home when she found she had to add to the family income. Callie, who worked as a beautician in a large shop for two years before her marriage, says she had always planned to wait until her two preschoolers were in school, then go back to work during their school hours. "However, we just couldn't make ends meet after our second baby was born. We talked about my husband's taking a night shift which would have paid more, or about his taking on a second job. But we were afraid if he did either of those things we would never have time for our family life.

"I didn't want to leave the kids to go out to work, so I decided to open a beauty shop in our basement. There aren't any beauty shops near here, so I knew there would be people coming to me."

Callie figured she could "get by" working only part time, so she established Fridays and Saturdays as her working days. Callie's husband spends Saturdays with their children. On Fridays, Callie discovered a clever way to work, to be near her children, to have them well cared for, and to provide care for the children of her customers. Callie pays a friend to run her "Friday Play School," which is adjacent to her beauty shop. (The basement of her tract home is divided into two rooms with accordion doors between. One half is Callie's shop, the other half is the children's playroom, where "Friday Play School" is held.)

"I encourage the mothers of preschoolers to schedule for Fridays and to bring their kids along. Then they don't have to get sitters and it's company for mine. I pay a friend to be with all the children, and if, in addition, the customers who bring kids want to pay her a little extra, that's fine, too. It's still cheaper for them, and easier than finding a sitter and leaving them at home, and it's more fun for everybody. You know, a lot of beauty shops don't like little kids coming and playing around during their mother's appointment. Mine is sure different.

"Financially, we can manage all right with my working part time now," Callie says. "Once the kids start school, I'll work more. Maybe I'll work in somebody else's shop during their school hours, or maybe I'll expand at home. I don't know. But right now I'm happy to be at home with the kids, and for the chance to earn enough at home so I can swing it."

Unlike Callie, who was motivated by financial necessity, Jeanette Morrison was moved by loneliness in a new community to turn her particular interest to special use at home. Before her marriage and for a year afterward, Jeanette taught high school French in a large city high school. "When I was pregnant, I was delighted. I planned to stop teaching after the baby was born and take some night school courses, hopefully toward a graduate degree. But that idea went by the wayside when, three months after our daughter Judy was born, my husband's job necessitated that we move here." ("Here" is a small midwestern town, over a hundred miles from a university.) "When we moved here three years ago, I decided to keep up with my French, and my teaching, and also to be at home with Judy. So, I started a conversational French class in my living room. In looking back, I think I also did it primarily because I was lonesome. Teaching in our home gave me a situation in which I was confident in our new locale. It was a great way to meet people, and I was able to feel a part of things, by doing something for them. I made many new friends that way.

"My classes met two afternoons a week, between one and three, while Judy napped. As she got older, she participated, too," Jeanette laughs. Now that Judy is in school full days, Jeanette teaches three classes a week, "beginners as well as those who have been with me to the point of being able to read and translate French history and literature." Because their town is located miles from a college or university, Jeanette has been able to provide a new interest and source of stimulation to many adults in her community who otherwise would have no way of taking such courses.

Like Jeanette, Nora Brydon used her background in a new way when she married and moved away from a large metropolitan area. "Right after I finished high school, I went to work as a salesgirl in the giftwear section of a department store," Nora says. "Three years later I was promoted to assistant buyer and was looking forward to making a career of merchandising. Then I met Bob, who owned and operated a six-hundred-acre farm over seventy-five miles from the nearest city. I married him a few months later, and a year after that was the mother of a baby boy. Those first couple of years really required a terrific adjustment, to marriage and motherhood, but most of all to life on a farm. I was happy with Bob and the baby, but I missed seeing other people—my next-door neighbor lived over a mile away!

"By the time the second baby came I realized I had to do something to keep in touch with the outside world, so I decided to bring part of it home. In preparation, I spent one whole spring painting and renovating a small, unused barn. Then I took a thousand dollars from the small bank account I had from my career-girl days to buy my initial merchandise, put some signs on the highway, advertised in the weekly that reaches nearby towns, and opened 'Nora's Gift House.' "

"All of a sudden, I had a business—albeit a very part-time business. Within a year, I added antiques, which I purchased from the owners of some of the old farmhouses around. Later, I began selling handicrafts done by some of the area residents. Word spread, and as years have gone by, I've gotten busier and busier.

"When I started out, people would come to our farmhouse when they wanted me; then, unless Bob was in the house, I'd take the kids to the store while my customer shopped. Now my son is in school all day, and our little girl is still at home with me. She accompanies me on 'buying trips' to neighboring farms, and goes over to the shop with me whenever customers come.

"It's funny," Nora reflects, "but I can hardly remember

when I used to find the farm such a lonely place. The very best thing about the shop is that I've made such good friends among people whom I originally met as customers."

While Nora's particular situation is unique, many women who have had careers in the bustling business world prior to beginning their families experience feelings of isolation in suburbia similar to those of Nora on the farm.

Annette Harding has a master's degree in business administration, and worked for a prestigious New York firm during the first three years of her marriage. "When I was visibly pregnant they made me begin my leave of absence. I fully intended to go back to work shortly after our baby was born, but when it came right down to it, I couldn't leave him. The thought of trading him for the long commute and all just didn't please me. But, being lonesome so much, out in the suburbs, didn't please me either.

"After a few months I decided if I set my mind to it, I could figure out a way to get a hand back in the business world, and keep my feet planted in our own home. And I have done so through doing private investment counseling."

Annette says all it took to get started was some letterhead stationery on which she wrote to friends, family, acquaintances, and former business contacts, stating her qualifications and her interest in helping them. "My business began slowly, which was fine. Knowing I had my hand in cheered me so I was more sociable and I became more involved with other young women who were also at home. Now, three years later, I have about twenty-five regular clients, whose portfolios I know well, and who call me for advice when they feel they need it. I review their situations here, at home, and do most of my work with them by telephone.

"Primarily, I help people who don't wish to change investments often, and who don't want to deal directly with brokers who might encourage more frequent trading. Yet, these people want to keep up with current developments, and not risk being caught short if interest rates change or the market drops.

"We have two children now, and are planning on more, so I don't want to take on many new clients in the foreseeable future. But I'm well into the field, I keep up on daily business, and I know that when the time comes, I can either do additional work at home, or get a good job outside home."

Phylis Everest also has a business background, and wished to pursue her special interest at home. Phylis was trained in accounting and worked in the comptroller's office of a large corporation until she left her job to begin her family. "At first I really wailed that there was no place for an organization woman except in an organization. I hardly felt that taking care of our small house, and my small child, required my business degree and work experience.

"After a period of feeling extremely sorry for myself, I decided to turn my training in a slightly new direction. When my baby was sleeping or playing quietly, I boned up to take the CPA exam. At first I didn't tell anyone, not even my husband, because I was afraid saying what I hoped to do would commit me irrevocably.

"Finally, I did tell, and did take the exam, and incredibly passed it the first time. From then on, doing taxes and other work was just a matter of making some of the people I knew in accounting firms aware that I was willing to help them—on my own time and here, at home."

Phylis hasn't wanted to take on nearly as much work as has been offered her during the past years, because of her family commitments. "It's funny—once I realized that nobody would paste a sign on me saying 'closed for the next twenty years' and that I could keep up right at home, I was able to figure out just what role I wanted my profession to play in my total life. And I must say that it's considerably less than I thought it would be.

"I organize things at home around the fact that I know I will do most of my accounting between the first of the year and April 15. I get extra cleaning help, extra sitters; cut down on volunteer activities and social life for that period of time; and do tax work about four hours a day. I work a couple of hours after the children go to bed at night, and the rest of the time during their nap and playtimes. It's a nice way to be part of the field, without having to lose out on the home front."

Each of these women, wishing to keep up with a specialty for which she was trained, was ingenious enough to find ways to do so without leaving her family. When a woman says she must leave home to use her specialty—that she is trained for something other (and usually the implication is "better") than being at home—what she frequently means is that she wishes to be away from home and is using her education or particular specialty as an excuse to do so. While such a woman is free to choose to leave her children to fill a prescribed niche in someone else's job categorization, she should not become a paradigm for *all* women who have education or specific training.

None of the women just discussed searched the want ads. Nor did they complain that their families were impeding their personal progress, that their husbands were oppressing them, that society was unfair. Each woman simply made use of her inner resources and ingenuity to see what she could do that others might need, and proceeded to create for herself a special niche.

This is definitely not to say that every woman should *utilize* a specialty rather than banking it. But it is to say that any woman who wishes to be at home with her family and to keep her hand in a special area of interest *can* without having to leave home to do it. Obviously, it is harder to make one's own place than to fill a vacancy in somebody else's hierarchy. But, it's also more challenging, and for a woman raising a family it can be more rewarding. For when a woman makes her own place it means she sets the timetable and specifications. It means she can pace herself to expand her own activities as her children grow older and are at home less. It means she can control her own activities so that she is free when her husband and children are free.

The question before every woman who desires to utilize a special interest or skill while she is raising her family is: Must I fill an existing niche, outside home, or is there a way I can redirect my specialty to work for me right there?

Vera Meyers and Kate Bradley both exemplify that a woman with training in medicine or other sciences can keep a place for herself in her respective field while at home raising a family, by making her own place. Similarly, Nora Brydon, Annette Harding, and Phylis Everest have shown that a woman can turn business education and experience to new use, while at home raising her family.

In the same way that Laura Evanson did, other women with training in various kinds of speech and reading problems could tutor at home. Tutoring individuals or teaching classes is one of the best ways a woman can both keep up in a field and build confidence in herself and her area of interest.

In this age of super-specialization, often the woman trained in a science, math, a language, or one of the arts says she would like to teach, but she doesn't have a degree. That should not stand in her way. We've all been subjected to teachers with college degrees and professors with Ph.D.s who are unable to communicate excitement about their disciplines, and we've all known persons with no degrees who are great educators. If a woman enjoys her specialty, wants to redirect it to work for her at home, and likes to communicate what she enjoys to others, she doesn't need a special label saying "teacher" to hang over her door in order to do it.

Kathryn Palmer wanted to keep up her interest in international relations and thought it would be fun to teach (she majored in Russian as an undergraduate, then did graduate work in international relations). Kathryn had no teaching experience, but encouraged by two of her neighbors who said they'd like to take a course from her, organized a group of friends and gave it a try. The participants agreed on a specific number of weeks and goals for the course. Kathryn taught strictly on a volunteer basis. "The class went very well," Kathryn says. "I was nervous at first, but after a couple of weeks I realized that my students were interested, and I relaxed and enjoyed discussions with them. I led several such groups as a volunteer, in our home, then. Now, I charge a small amount per person for an hour-a-week, six-week course. Recently, I was asked to teach outside home, in an adult education program in our community center. I'll only be doing it once a week this year, because my children are still home during the day, but it's something to look forward to doing more of when they're in school. I also plan to finish up my graduate work at that time. Teaching has helped me to keep up my own interest in international relations, and I've learned a lot on my own to teach it that I didn't seek to learn as a student."

Any kind of history, social science, or literature course can be taught in one's home. So can any language, including English. A friend of ours gets great satisfaction and makes many interesting new friends through teaching English to foreign students and their families, in her own living room.

Many women teach various kinds of arts and crafts—such as water-coloring, macramé, crocheting, needlepoint—in their own living rooms or family rooms; other women enjoy giving cooking classes of all kinds, in their kitchens. Ethnic cooking and specialty foods are very popular both with the women who give the classes and the men, women, and teen-agers who take them.

In addition to the immediate satisfaction that teaching a specialty at home gives, a woman gains experience which qualifies her for other kinds of teaching and uses of her specialty when her children are older. Her experience transfers to "Y"s, extended-day programs in grade and high schools, and adult education programs. It also transfers to teaching in center-city youth programs, alternative education programs, such as open and free schools, and higher education alternatives, such as "colleges without walls."

Teaching is only one means of redirecting an interest to keep it alive and functioning while a woman is at home raising a family. There are many other ways in which a woman can create a niche for her interest, tailoring it to her priority of being at home.

A woman talented in art may have worked for an ad agency or done ads for a retail store; as a woman at home she is free to use her interest when and how she chooses. She can sketch and paint for her own enjoyment; she may have her walls—and the walls of her friends and family—hung with her works. She may begin to show and sell her paintings, or she may do free-lance illustrating. One woman I talked with began part-time, at-home free-lancing by illustrating the Ph.D. thesis of a friend who was doing a project on children's ads.

A woman with an interest in philosophy, humanities, or literature may have filled a position in a publishing firm or library; at home there are dozens of positions she can create for herself. She can lead a Great Books group, either an existing one or form her own. Or she might begin book reviewing. Many small community or suburban newspapers have no staff reviewers, and because they may have too few personnel for too many jobs, often "reviews" are merely excerpts from publisher's blurbs. Many an editor is glad to find a critical free-lance reviewer to give independent views. Libraries often put out weekly, monthly, or semi-yearly sheets or brochures on current books. Writing reviews for one of them is a good way to keep sharp critical reading skills.

Frequently, women who have developed ways to use a special interest, training, or talent at home become models for other women, newly beginning families. Shirley Wells, a young woman expecting her first baby, says, "I'd always planned to keep teaching while raising a family. Until recently I couldn't imagine staying home. But I have some very bright and interesting friends who are home raising their families, and are active and involved in lots of things while they're there. It's inspired me. I'm as excited now about starting a family and having a chance to try my hand at some of my own projects as I was about starting college ten years ago."

Shirley enjoys teaching and deeply regrets leaving. "But I don't want to work and let somebody else raise my child. I want to do that myself. And I'm also looking forward to trying some things on my own. So far, my job has been very secure, and staying with it, I suppose, would be easier on my ego than what may lie ahead. Now, who knows what will come of my ideas and plans? I want to do a lot more macramé, possibly teach it at home, maybe sell my work. And one thing I've wanted to do for years and haven't had the chance to is to learn to weave. I also want to take pottery courses and become a really good potter. And to expand the calligraphy I do for fun, perhaps into a business doing wedding announcements and invitations.

"Now, I certainly don't expect to attempt all this the first year. But, it's a long list of things I want to try, to learn, to do, during the time I'm home raising my children. With a list like this, I don't think I'll ever get bored!"

6

Ms. Jekyll and Mrs. Hyde

MAKING TIME

How can a woman make time for her own individual pursuits—be they reading a book, developing a creative outlet, or
utilizing a specialty at home—and prevent these pursuits from
interfering with her family life? How can she do so without
feeling like Ms. Jekyll and Mrs. Hyde?

Every woman at home is involved in some activities which
do *not* directly concern her family. To make time for her own
endeavors she must first evaluate all those activities which do
not directly pertain to her family and decide which of them are
self-imposed, and which are imposed upon her. If an activity is
self-imposed—a committee or volunteer activity, for example—a
woman may wish to make more time for it. If it is imposed
upon her, if she just drifted into it, and she doesn't enjoy it, she
can well eliminate it to make more room in her life for those
activities which do interest her.

Since in success-ethic terms, the woman at home, regardless
of how busy she is with her family and personal pursuits, is
thought to be "doing nothing," requests for her to serve on
committees or collect for worthy causes are always coming in.
And they will continue to until she makes the decision that
what she is doing at home is as valuable as what a man or
woman working outside home is doing, and that her time is
equally valuable. Once she is confident of that, she will explain
in the same way that she would if she were working outside

home, to those who make requests which she does not care to fulfill, that her time is already allocated. This is not to say that a woman at home should not volunteer her time and energies for projects which interest her. But she must free herself from the projects that don't, in order to make the time for the activities that do.

This attitude must be applied to requests from working mothers to baby-sit, drive their children various places, and to care for them when ill. Mothers who choose to work, and who have not made appropriate arrangements for their children, often heap such requests on their neighbors who prefer to be at home. For example, Marla Tolen and her neighbor Florence both have grade-schoolers, and each has a kindergarten-age child. Marla drives her kindergartener to and from school each morning. Florence took a morning job and asked Marla if she would also drive her son to school as her work schedule prohibited her from doing it herself. Marla was glad to help Florence out. When Florence began asking Marla to keep her son for a few minutes extra on the return trip, "until she could get home," Marla obliged. When the few minutes began to run regularly anywhere from half an hour to an hour and a half each day, Marla felt misused.

"I also plan to do some part-time work," Marla says, "but I intend to wait until my daughter is in school all day. This year I stayed at home so I could spend lunch time and the early afternoon with her before the other children come home. This is our special time together to do what the two of us want to do. Sometimes we invite another mother and child over to lunch with us, sometimes my daughter brings a friend home from school, other times she and I read, or bake together. Florence's little boy is a nice kid, and I don't mind having him here occasionally, but having him on a daily basis restricts the things my daughter and I do. I told Florence how I felt and asked that either she be here on time from now on or that she make other arrangements for her son. Florence became very angry and said she didn't see why I wouldn't help her as long as I'm 'just at home anyway.' "

This situation is a dramatic example of the fact that while a woman at home may be glad to help a friend in a pinch, if the pinches recur too often, it's obvious that the absentee mother simply hasn't bothered to make adequate arrangements for her family, but rather assumes that a neighbor who's "just home anyway" will fill in for her. This attitude arises in part from the women's lib philosophy which postulates that some persons are better able than others to raise children. While everyone should breed children, if they wish, the argument goes, some should specialize in raising them, while others work outside home. That assumption rests on the notion that everyone has a specialty, and that the woman at home is specializing in day-care. It presumes that because a woman chooses to be at home raising her own children, she would like to make a career of raising children in general. Yet, most women who choose to be at home aren't at all interested in making a career of raising children other than in their own family, and therefore, do not wish to have their homes become drop-off centers for the children of neighbors who choose to work outside their own homes.

By culling from her life those activities which do not pertain to her family and which give her no pleasure, a woman makes time for her "own thing." A woman's personal activities can take many forms, and the time she has to devote to them varies considerably between Phase One and Phase Two, and varies again between Phases Two and Three.

Phase One

The woman who chooses to take on another interest at home during Phase One can do so effectively provided that (1) she is relaxed enough about what she's doing so she doesn't view her children as interference, and (2) she realizes she can count on only short periods of uninterrupted time to do her own thing.

This approach runs contrary to the dogma which states that a woman's personal pursuits seek and deserve expression just as surely as her children seek and deserve to grow, and therefore justifies a woman's taking large blocks of time from her family for her own endeavors.

The woman who goes beyond this view does not choose to

create a situation for self-expression which says, "It's them or me." Being with her children during their growing years is her first priority, not out of duty or self-sacrifice, but out of the desire to enjoy her children's early years with them to the fullest.

As long as a woman remembers her priorities, and works her personal activities around children's nap time or quiet playtimes—and does this without resenting them for waking up early or playing loudly—she'll not feel like Jekyll and Hyde. "There are two ways to look at merging personal activities with raising a family," Rita Pauling says. "One leads to frustration, the other to a sense of accomplishment. If I felt that my primary commitment was to my sculpting, then I'd be in a state of constant frustration because of the time the family took from it. But, obviously, I don't feel that way. My family is my first commitment; I've chosen it that way. So I feel a great sense of accomplishment in that I've found personal rewards through my sculpting, without feeling I've sacrificed time with my family to do it. I think a woman must know her priorities, and must set realistic expectations, in order to enjoy other interests while raising a family. There's no point in planning to do too much in any one day. Better let it be a surprise to get more done than you expected, rather than constantly feeling you haven't done as much as you'd hoped."

Women who do their own thing at home while raising preschoolers agree that in addition to knowing their priorities and setting realistic goals, they must learn to function with interruptions, on a stop-and-start basis. "I had always believed that an artistic individual had to be cloistered in a garret in order to work creatively," Kathy Jacovi laughs. "Boy, have I learned differently. I stop and start a sketch or a watercolor a dozen times a day, some days. What's amazing to me is that I do as much as I do. Having developed my interest in art under these conditions, who knows what I'll be able to accomplish when I have a prolonged period of time for it!"

Phase Two

Often a woman who hasn't experienced the need before, be-

gins to yearn for "something else" once her children are all in
school. At first it may take the form of a vague emptiness trig-
gered by the frequent question from friends and acquaintances
—"What are you doing now?" Or it may hit hard the first Sep-
tember day that all the children troop out the door—and
nobody comes home at noon.

"All of a sudden," as one woman put it, "it's the beginning
of a new era."

"But don't get fooled," another woman, whose children have
all been in school for several years, quickly chimes in. "It's not
all the time it seems."

Both are right. When the youngest child is off to school, a
new era does begin; there is more time, but it is not nearly as
much as it seems. And this accounts for a great deal of frustration among women who haven't decided how much time they
actually have to do "something else," and what they want that
"something else" to be.

For the dilemma that many women face at this juncture in
their lives is: there doesn't seem to be much point in being at
home, alone with no other commitment when the family isn't
there, but what kind of other commitment will allow being at
home when the family is? Staying at home waiting for others to
come home can be lonely for a woman—yet if she takes a job
outside home there may be a lot of time that her children will
have to wait at home, lonely for her.

Before taking on other commitments, it's important for her
to assess how much time she really has available to get done
what she feels must be done in the house—to keep it organized
and running—and to reserve some very personal time to feel
refreshed when her family comes home later in the day.

If her children are in school say, from nine to three, five days
a week, that thirty hours a week may seem like a great deal of
time. However, once she subtracts from that the time she needs
for household matters and also time she would like to keep as
free time for herself—to read a book, talk with a neighbor, or
have lunch with an old friend—there may be substantially less
than thirty hours left.

She also must keep in mind that children are not in school

during the summer, during winter vacation, spring vacation, over Thanksgiving weekend, for various state and national holidays and teachers' meetings. In addition, she needs to estimate realistically how many days each child might miss from school because of illness.

What she actually has available for other commitments, when all is assessed, is perhaps fifteen or twenty hours a week about three quarters of the year. She is then faced with the same kind of decision she made when she initially decided to stay at home and raise her children, only it's not so clear-cut. When she was home with her preschoolers, anything else she took on was quite obviously an "addition to" her major commitment. If she was active in the community, did volunteer work, took a course, or pursued an interest as a part-time job from home, it was evident to her and to the others with whom she was involved that this was in a very real sense extra-curricular.

But, in Phase Two, the lines are not so clearly drawn, and it's easy for priorities to become obscured if a woman overestimates the time she has available for things outside her family.

For instance, if she takes a year-round half-time job, it may seem that she has plenty of time for everything else, but she may quickly find herself stretched. Besides that, come the first school vacation, she may realize she's not so happy being at work half-days while the children are at home with a baby-sitter. Or, if she has children in a wide age range, she may find that her expectations of her fourteen-year-old being responsible for her nine- and seven-year-olds while she's at the office were unrealistically high.

She may suddenly find herself a "working mother," even though she's only at her job half time. That half of the time may stretch many of her days beyond what is comfortable, may detract from her family life, and may force her into many of the same binds of the full-time working mother: having to arrange for child care during school vacations, missing the fun of being with her children during that time, and finding that she's tired out and craves time by herself.

Bonnie Larson is one woman who discovered this. Bonnie

did legal secretarial work before her marriage and decided to take a half-time job in the fall when all her children were in school full days for the first time. Her office hours were from nine to one, Monday through Friday, in a downtown office twenty minutes by freeway from her home. "I thought it would be neat to get back into an office again, and that I'd get some shopping done while I was out. My hours were good because I'd leave home when the family did and get home—even with shopping—an hour before the children did."

Bonnie says it was fun—for a couple of weeks. "Then I began to get resentful of the job . . . just going every day, and of the family, because I couldn't fit in all my other activities around theirs. So I knew I had to either drop everything else, or quit the job." (Bonnie is active in PTA, plays the piano in a civic orchestra, and participates in other community activities.)

"All of a sudden I realized that my personal pursuits had become pretty important to me, and I didn't want to give them all up—obviously I wasn't going to shortchange the family, so it had to be the job."

Bonnie talked over the problem with her employer, who suggested that she try working at home on a part-time basis instead. "That changed the whole picture. I go in once or twice a week, pick up the tapes, draft and then retype the briefs at home, and then bring them into the office. This is the perfect compromise. I now do the work on my own time, and often I do most of it during the morning when I would have been in the office anyway. But my attitude is different. I don't feel chained to a schedule; I can spend the same after-school time with the children I always did, and it's no hassle when one of them is home with the flu or something. I don't have to arrange last-minute sitters or be down at the office worrying about leaving them alone at home."

Bonnie points out an oft-cited problem: "Just because the children are all in grade school—or high school—doesn't mean that you're no longer needed on the home front. I think my own experience shows that it's easy to overcommit yourself outside your family, thinking, 'Well, they don't need me so much now, anyway.'"

Most mothers who have active households and who enjoy being with their families find they are *busier* with family life as their children get older than they were when the children were younger. Many mothers of teen-agers report their number-one role in interacting with their teen-agers is that of sounding board. As Elaine Sanderson, a mother of four sons, ages ten to nineteen, explains: "They want your time, and privately. Each one wants a little time each day for himself. I want to be there to listen, not all harassed from my own busy day. That's why I always take a nap and reading break between my busy mornings and the time the family arrives. Also the day gets longer—the whole family is up and active well into the evening; whereas we used to put the kids to bed at seven when they were little, now things are still jumping at eleven."

While home is less busy earlier in the day, the action goes on *later* as the children get older. If a mother fills her days to the bursting point with a half-time job ("as long as they're in school anyway") she often finds it, like a full-time job, more a strain than a freedom. She then has to push every other activity she enjoys, every small domestic responsibility, all her family life, into the same after-school hours.

When a woman assesses her time and interests, deciding whether to use them for a half-time job outside home or not, the real question for her to keep in mind is, "How can I use this interest (the "career" and "profession" connotations are just formalized descriptions of an existing interest) in such a way as to get the most from it without its interfering with my family and with other personal activities?"

This kind of evaluation makes clear the advantages of a woman's creating a part-time job of her own design. It's important that every woman realize that there is a big difference between a *part-time job of her own design,* and a *part-time* or *half-time job.* A *part-time* or *half-time job* is one where an employer designates the duties and specifies a certain number of hours per week (frequently twenty hours per week because that is half of the usual forty-hour work week). In contrast, a *part-time job of a woman's own design* is one in which she specifies what she will do and when she will do it. This kind of job may take two hours a week, or ten. The timing is flexible to meet her personal timetable. Much or all of it can be done at home, because the specifications as well as the timing are her own. That way she can ease up, or not work at all, during school vacations, allocate her work so that she is done long before the children arrive home from school, and she's right there if someone wakes up in the morning with 102° fever. She doesn't have to cancel appointments, worry about an irate boss, call a neighbor, or all three.

There are not a host of readily available niches outside home into which the bright, energetic woman, who does not want to compromise her family life, can fit. But, there are, as we've seen in the preceding sections, infinite ways in which a bright, energetic woman who does not want to compromise her family can create a niche for herself right *at* home.

For instance, when her children are in school, a woman is free to take a block of discretionary time which was previously unavailable to her to pursue a new or an existing interest. However, it is crucial that she first evaluate her total time, then see how she can make the best use of it to ensure that her activities are a source of joy rather than a pressure to her and to her family.

Amelia Fraley discovered an effective means of utilizing her Phase Two time. "When I married, had a baby, and we moved from New York to Atlanta, I closed the door on my career as a fashion designer. I haven't designed clothes since, except for myself and our five children. But I've refinished a lot of furniture, done the centerpieces and decorations for more of the children's school affairs and our church functions than I can count, and I've found out I can work with a palette and a knife.

"When I was single and career-minded, I never thought of painting. In fact, I didn't paint until the last of our brood started first grade—that was ten years ago. When five children came in nine years, there was a period where I just didn't have the time to concentrate. But when they were all in school, then I did begin painting every morning. I let the breakfast dishes sit, the desk pile high, the phone ring. I didn't care. I figured the children were my major responsibility and with them gone from home for almost seven hours a day, I decided to take one half that time for myself. I wanted to try painting seriously and see if I could do it.

"I also started taking lessons, and even though I'm presently selling over fifty paintings a year, I still do. There is always more to learn.

"Now, with almost all the children grown—we have only two at home and they are in college—I have a great deal of time to devote to my art, and I love it. But I'm glad I didn't try to divide myself in the earlier years. I enjoyed all the children when they were home; now I enjoy this. And when the grandchildren come, I lock up my studio—one of the extra bedrooms is now my sunny place to paint—and play with them."

Amelia is one of many women who has taken advantage of Phase Two to accomplish something she really wanted to do, and, thereby, to prepare herself for the time when the children all leave home. Her method of implementing her desire to do her thing is one that might work well for other women. When she says, "I leave the breakfast dishes, let the desk pile high, let the phone ring," she is expressing the fact that she puts her own personal interest above details of household management. "Once I've spent the morning in my studio," Amelia says, "I find it relaxing to clean up the kitchen, pay the bills, make calls, do all the little things that would be an intrusion on 'my time' at nine in the morning."

Amelia's situation exemplifies the principle that in order to have an uninterrupted period of time for her own thing, a woman must critically evaluate just how much total time she has available, then organize that time in the way that proves most effective for her.

Like Amelia, Judy Maynard has carefully organized her time to suit her own needs. Judy, who has a degree in library science, indexes books and manuscripts on an independent basis. "I work at the dining room table from about ten to noon or one every day. But as soon as everyone is out the door in the morning, I clean up and get the household business out of the way. I am very quick because I don't like to get a late start at my own work, so I hurry through the tedium around the house to get at what's important to me. When I'm done indexing, except on Tuesdays, I'm free until the children get home.

"That one afternoon a week is for grocery shopping and other errands. I keep a list, and only shop once a week; that way I don't mess up my other days. But the other afternoons I'm free to meet friends for lunch or coffee; to help out at the community center with a golden-age program, something I'm very interested in; or just to stay home and read or sew."

Chris Elliot has also organized her time to meet both her personal needs and the needs of her family. One of thousands of women across the country who have made similar decisions, Chris started college when her youngest child entered first grade. Chris, who married her high school sweetheart the day after graduation and began her family a year later, believes, "This is the best stage of life at which to go to school. And I'm benefiting by going slowly. I take one or two courses a quarter instead of the usual three or four or even five classes taken by full-time students. This way, I can 'dig into' each course. I do a lot of additional reading for each one because I don't have to cram lots of varying subjects into every quarter."

Chris keeps to a three-day-a-week class schedule, and takes only morning classes. "This means I must omit some things I'd really like to take, or that I have to wait until another quarter when they're offered at a better time. But you can't have everything. There are plenty of new and interesting courses to choose from that meet my needs. I go to class Monday, Wednesday, and Friday mornings. Monday and Wednesday afternoons I study in the library until it's time to pick my younger two children up at school. On those days I do nothing in the house, except make breakfast and dinner.

"Tuesday and Thursday mornings I stay home, run loads of laundry while I'm studying, and pick up in the house when I need stretch-breaks. Tuesday, Thursday and Friday afternoons before the children get home are free for tennis, for having coffee with friends, and things like that. The kids help me do most of the cleaning on Saturday mornings, and what doesn't get done, doesn't get done.

"School is terrific as a complement to my life, but I wouldn't let hurrying for a degree take me over. Even at this pace, I'll have my B.A. about the time our youngest son starts high school. College has added a great deal to my life, and because I'm going slowly, it's not taking anything away."

Phase Three

The challenge of keeping her family in primary focus while enjoying her own activities does not cease once a woman enters Phase Three. Family life is not over, yet the time for a woman's personal activities is at its peak. The question of the Phase Three woman is not, "How can I squeeze in enough personal time?" but rather, "How can I make the best use of my increased free time, while enjoying these years with my husband, and staying in close touch with my grown family?" There is no "right" and "only" norm for a woman to follow during this stage of her life, but there is a wide range of options open to her: some women choose to take full-time jobs, others work part-time outside home, while still others expand or continue their interests at home. Some women choose to return to school at this time; others increase or begin participation in community ventures. Many women combine two or more of these options at various times during this period of their lives. Whatever choices a Phase Three woman makes, one thing is clear: the woman who has kept her family in high priority during Phases One and Two most often continues to do so at this juncture in her life.

Fifty-seven-year-old Georgia Peterson both directs a suburban adult education program, a job which she describes as "challenging and time-consuming," and spends a great deal of time with her husband and grown children. Georgia, who took adult education courses while her children were small, began teaching classes when her children were older, and was made director of the program four years ago, after her children were no longer living at home. "The timing was good," Georgia says. "The job was offered me three months before our youngest daughter's wedding and I said 'okay,' if they'd wait for me until after the wedding, which they did. Actually, I had been offered the position once before and turned it down. I still had two children living at home, and it would have been too much for me to work full time, then. But now, it's perfect."

Now that her children aren't at home, Georgia has more time with her husband. "We play golf together on Saturdays, have dinner out a couple of nights a week, and often go to movies or concerts. I am highly organized at home, because two of our four children and their families live within twenty minutes of us, and we encourage them to drop over to eat with us on the weekends, and occasionally during the week, too. And, of course, we have Thanksgiving, Christmas, and all the birthday celebrations at home, for everybody in the family.

"I'm very aware that my kind of schedule is not for every woman," Georgia adds. "I require very little sleep and have always been blessed with exceedingly good health and a great deal of energy. Otherwise, I couldn't do all that I do and enjoy it."

While Georgia thrives on the combination of her full-time job and her continued close family relationships, Ellen Michaels is equally enthusiastic about her college course-work and personal life. "There is definitely more time now that neither of our daughters is at home any longer," Ellen says. "I have only my husband and myself to plan for on a day-to-day basis. When our youngest daughter left home three years ago, I was really at loose ends for a while. I'd worked as a secretary for a couple of years before our marriage but I didn't care to return to office work. What I'd always wanted to do was to go to college, but I felt that I was too old. Finally, my husband convinced me that I couldn't lose anything by trying. So I did. At forty-five, I was a college freshman, taking a full load, and commuting over an hour each way to school. Now, I'm beginning my junior year, and wondering how I ever considered not going to school. These past two years have been terribly happy, busy ones. I've commuted to classes at least three days every week, some semesters four and even five days."

Ellen's husband has taken an avid interest in her courses, many of which are in philosophy and anthropology. "Since he had a business background a lot of this is as new to him as it is to me. When I write papers, he talks with me about what I'm doing; when I study for exams he frequently reads some of the material and quizzes me.

"School has also worked out in terms of our personal plans because he now has a month a year of vacation, which we take during the summer. After I finish my schooling, I'll find some use for my education which won't entail full-time work. If I were to work full time, I'd be just starting out, and it's unlikely that I could get as much vacation as he does, or necessarily get it at the same time. It would bog us down just at a time in our lives when we're freer."

Ellen believes that another advantage of being in school is that her schedule "has not interfered with seeing my married daughters. One of them lives several hundred miles from us and she and her family visit during my school vacations. When her baby was born last winter, I got advance assignments from my professors and went out to stay with her older children while she was in the hospital.

"Our other daughter lives only half an hour from us. She and her family frequently come for dinner, and her wonderful little boy spends quite a lot of time with me. He usually comes over for the day on Saturday, and sometimes I pick him up in the afternoons on my way home from school; he stays for supper, and then his parents come over to take him home."

Tina Malloy is another Phase Three woman, busy with her own activities, and closely involved with her family as well. Tina has a plant shop in the sunroom of her home, appropriately called "The Green Thumb," which developed as an outgrowth of plant care she did for her neighbors. "I always had the sunroom full of greenery while my neighbors would complain that nothing would grow for them. I would show them a few tricks, and as their luck improved, they'd come to me with other plant questions, or for new slips. Some of them started buying my plants from me, and then bringing the plants back here when they went out of town, or when the plants weren't doing too well."

After Tina's children began school, two of her neighbors volunteered to help her get started in business. One neighbor designed a flyer for her which was mailed out to everyone Tina and she knew. Another neighbor wrote ads for the local newspapers.

"The Green Thumb" has grown over the years both in number of customers and in the services Tina offers. She sells plants of many kinds, offers a consultation service on caring for them, and "plant-sits" for traveling customers whose plants require special care. Two years ago Tina, a frequent speaker at garden club meetings, began giving a course called "Personalities of Plants" at her suburb's community center. "The course got going so well that I'm also giving it in two adjacent communities."

Everything Tina does personally is flexible enough so that it doesn't conflict with time she enjoys spending with her husband and with their grown family. "Our single son lives in the city so he comes home very often, but our two married daughters live hundreds of miles from us," Tina says. "Each one, with her husband and children, comes to visit us at separate times every year. For part of each visit, we treat them and ourselves to a special kind of vacation. We give each daughter and her husband a check to go away by themselves for a few days, and we keep the children. It's nice for everybody concerned, but I think my husband Ken and I benefit the most. It's hard having grandchildren living away; we want to be more a part of their lives than just pictures and voices on the phone. So having them all to ourselves even for a few days a year helps.

"Ken and I also go to visit each daughter and her family at least once a year. Using his vacation to see them means we don't take the kinds of trips we'd always thought we would. But, how can seeing the South of France compare with visiting our grandson in Pittsburgh?"

Seventy-one-year-old Agnes Revne is another woman who both enjoys a job where she works with others and maintains a continued concern for her family. Agnes, who works part-time on the sales floor of a popular suburban bookstore says, "I've been working here for the past fifteen years, ever since my son and daughter got married. When there were no longer any kids at home, I decided to get out of the house and be with people.

I work Mondays and Fridays all year, every day during the Christmas rush, and fill in at other times when the place is really hopping.

"I stayed at home full time when my kids were at home, and even after they left I never wanted to work full time, because if something comes up with one of them or with the grand-kids, then I like to be there. You don't stop being a parent, you know, just because the kids aren't living under your roof any more. And, when my husband had an operation last year, I didn't work for three months. I just took off, stayed home, and kept him company while he convalesced."

While some Phase Three women find part-time jobs outside home a real addition to their lives, others have no desire to allocate their time in this way. "Good Lord," says fifty-two-year-old Brenda Fairchild, whose three children are living away from home, "why should I want to go out to work at this stage of my life? We don't need the money, and I don't need a job in order to keep busy.

"My husband's an executive with a lot of responsibility, and now that the children are gone, I go on business trips with him. He travels frequently and there's no way I could pick up and leave even a part-time job on the hit-and-miss basis going with him entails.

"I like to do a lot of things around home, too—gardening, needlepoint, and I play the flute in our community orchestra. Also, I play a lot of golf, and swim at least twice a week.

"Our son and daughter come home from college every vacation, and get jobs here during the summers. I like being around when they're here. A lot of kids don't come home very much; and I'm flattered that ours do. It's nice to know that you've done a good enough job raising your family that they seek you out once they're no longer under the same roof."

Alberta Gunderson is similarly enthusiastic about the balance of her personal relationships and personal time. Alberta, who lives in a Milwaukee suburb, says, "We've a son in the Peace Corps in North Africa, two daughters working on the West Coast, and our youngest son is stationed in Hawaii. I miss them terribly, but we write and phone them often, and my husband and I manage to see each of the ones in the U.S. at least once a year; either they come here or we go there. Last year, we spent his vacation with three of the children. Both of our girls took time off. We met them in San Francisco, then we all flew to Hawaii.

"This year both of our daughters will be home for Christmas, and if our son is still there, we're going to North Africa in the spring. Now that none of the four lives at home, my husband and I do a lot of things together which we didn't when they were growing up. We have been taking some evening classes together, and we have taken up bridge.

"I've been on the board of a children's hospital for many years, but now I have been volunteering two afternoons a week there, to work with the children. I read to some, and just talk with others. We began a poetry group for some of them who are there on a long-term convalescent basis. Working with these children helps make up for having no children at home any more, and no grandchildren on the scene, as yet."

Each of these Phase Three women who has stayed at home to raise her family disproves the notion that the woman who makes this choice will have nothing left when her children leave home but endless empty hours. On the contrary, each of these women makes happy, constructive use of her abilities and interests while she keeps personal relationships in high priority. Not surprisingly, each speaks of having more time, during this period of her life, to enjoy with her husband. And each speaks of keeping in close touch, and seeing frequently, her grown children and in many cases her grandchildren.

Talking with many of these women reminded me of my husband's Grandma Bess, who made the most of her family relationships and her personal time until she was past ninety-five.

When she was over sixty, and already widowed for some years, Gram was persuaded by her two daughters, both of whom lived in Minneapolis, to move there from Syracuse. Grandma immediately made new friends, and was a sought-after guest at parties given not only by her daughters, but by their friends, and as they grew up, by her grandchildren. She was a highly gifted storyteller and conversationalist; a widely read self-educated woman who knew about many subjects. Grandma loved plays, concerts, lectures, and was an avid bridge player.

Although she was busy, Grandma had time for everyone in the family. When apples were plentiful, she'd make applesauce for all the grandchildren. Sometimes she'd call and say, "Come by for lunch, I've got some tapioca pudding ready" (the wonderful homemade kind of tapioca she knew I remembered from my childhood when my Grandma Mary made it for me). Or she'd bring a jar of her own freshly made orange marmalade when she came for dinner. When someone in the family was sick she was always there to help out, even as we cautioned her that she should stay away lest she catch the illness. "I never get sick," she'd laugh, and she didn't.

At ninety-plus, Grandma Bess was still an integral part of family life while staying personally active. At her ninety-second birthday party, she asked, "Will you drive me over to the campus tomorrow?" "Sure, Gram," I answered, "but why?" "Well, I'd like to sit in on a class there," she replied. "I always like to learn a little something new."

7

The Making of a Family

The woman who chooses not only to marry and have children, but to stay at home to make a home—has recognized, either consciously or unconsciously, her own need for human companionship, for love, understanding, and for a place of belonging. She desires to be a part of something other than herself, to form something larger and longer lasting than herself. She chooses not merely to perpetuate the species by having children, but to continue the human race, by helping her children to become compassionate, sensitive human beings.

Implementing this desire within a culture whose norms appear to hold material success in higher esteem than human values is a difficult matter. For the woman who chooses to make a family today has before her a tremendous challenge: instilling in her children compassion for others, providing them with the inner security to contribute concern and sensitivity to the world beyond themselves, imbuing them with humanistic values in a mechanistic social order, giving them a feeling of belonging to something greater than themselves—their family, their community, their world.

The woman who works every day to meet this challenge realizes that the way to make a home life of which each family member feels a vital part is to make time for it. There is no other way. If the family—and the individual within the context of the family—is to survive, it needs time to grow. The nuclear family of today has particular problems, for it has no ready-made frame of reference into which to fit. The nuclear family requires time not only for self-growth, but also to extend itself through drawing others into its sphere. Just as the individual is a link in the chain of humanity, so is the family a link to other families, other individuals, and institutions.

As our social and technological order increases in complexity, creating a home and family life becomes more difficult and demanding. The house can either be a home or it can be the residence of several family members of varying ages and interests, each of whom may be on a different time schedule, each living a separate alienated existence.

A home wherein close human relationships and feelings of security are developed and nurtured is one where family members share a sense of belonging. Families that are the happiest are those that place a high premium on their home lives. These are families in whose homes members feel a deep concern for one another; where they seek one another out; where they sit down and talk with one another; where they eat meals together; share weekends, evening and holiday times; where their friends drop in; where an aura of "this is the place I most want to be" prevails.

Such a home doesn't just happen, but rather is created through the conscious effort of persons who care—about themselves, about one another, about the future of their world. A happy, secure home atmosphere is woven from feelings of caring and loving, human intangibles which are necessary ingredients for warm, enduring relationships. Such relationships are established with a mate, and with each child from birth, then nurtured as the entire family grows.

These relationships are nourished through rhythms of continuous communication and activity among members of the family on a daily, weekly, and yearly basis. In families where the woman chooses to be at home, these rhythms include: the woman interacting with her preschoolers throughout the day; the woman being at home when children return home from school, talking with and listening to them; parents spending some individual time each week with each child; the family eating at least one meal a day together; families spending weekend and vacation time together, celebrating holidays and traditions; extending the family to others—other families, other children.

The succeeding three chapters will discuss the various means of implementing these time rhythms on a daily, weekly, and yearly basis.

8

Bridging the Generation Gap

The generation gap begins in the cradle. It doesn't suddenly happen. A woman can avoid it by pacing her life so that she can communicate with her children every step of the way.

The period of time when the children are small—while they are babies, toddlers, preschoolers—is the period in which the foundation for their lives is built. It is during this time that their basic sense of security is developed and nurtured, during this time that children develop the ability to communicate and respond.

This can be an especially difficult period for the woman who is previously inexperienced with children, and who may, in addition, be away from old friends, and relatives, with no one to turn to for ideas and advice. (It's not surprising that day-care—someone else to take the responsibility—frequently sounds appealing to the new mother.)

Until recent decades, children were simply absorbed into the extended-family structure. There a new mother had *her* mother and often sisters, aunts, and in-laws as well, to guide her. There were so many others around to give her help and advice—at times an overabundance—that she had automatic built-in group support for her efforts. As a new mother she didn't feel isolated or lonely, but rather was immediately a part of a group structure wherein she and her child had a secure place.

She was able to gain confidence in her new role gradually. But today the "instant motherhood" of our mobile culture is a fact of many women's lives, and with it comes the need for the same kind of spirit and confidence of the pioneer woman.

In a very real sense, the woman who opts for staying home to raise her children today is breaking new ground. No longer a part of an extended family wherein her role is clearly defined, wherein she has strong models and an already established sense of direction for her own life and the lives of her children, she is on her own. In addition, she is a part of a culture which has come to deify the functions which a woman may perform outside the home—but which has placed raising a family in lower priority.

The woman who leaves her children with others in order to work away from home often does so because she does *not* feel qualified to be at home with her children. So she says, "I'll be bored at home," or "I need to work away from the house and kids; I feel lonely at home." Yet she never gets to the root of why it may be boring, or why—amid those closest to her—she feels lonely; she never gets down to the fact that she simply doesn't feel as confident or as qualified with her children as she does on a job for which she has training and/or a college degree.

Such a woman needs the confidence to realize that there is no one better qualified to care for her children than she is. She needs to recover from the notion that somehow there are experts or authorities in child care who can give her children something she can't. That's just a "fadditude" caused and perpetuated by our current mania for specialization.

If a woman has worked as a secretary, or a lawyer, or a medical technician, or a doctor, she often believes that work to be her major function, her life. She may also believe a teacher is someone with special talents along the lines of child care, who can better care for her child than she can. So she believes she should go to an office and pound the typewriter, or plead her case, or give a test, while her child goes elsewhere to learn about life and living from someone she's never met or barely knows.

Obviously, when a mother *must* work so her children can eat, then day-care, nursery schools, and extended-day programs fill an important need in providing a place off the streets where children can participate in activities together. But this is in no way a replacement for home life, for the kind of one-to-one relationship between mother and child that can only be fostered at home over many days and years. Where mothers are lucky enough not to have to work to meet the physical needs of the family—but work instead for other reasons—mother and child may well lose in the long run.

Certainly the woman who can't spare the time to stay home with her child for the first few years of his life can't expect to develop the same kind of rapport with him that she would over a long-term, hour-by-hour, day-by-day basis. And because she can always work later, but a child will only be a child for a little while, it seems wholly worth while for every mother to evaluate not only her feelings at the moment, but to look to the future as well. For if she wants to be close to her child throughout her life, she must provide him with a feeling of closeness at the start of his life.

Human children are the most creative, explorative, daring, innovative creatures on earth. Some women privileged to be not only custodians of their bodies, but of their minds, have often not been able to cope with the challenge. So they use a whole host of institutions to do it for them—everything from day-care centers (quality controlled) to nursery schools, extended-day programs, and early entrance to college.

And while schools—to a point—are good, and necessary, abrogating the responsibility for raising one's own children to those "trained" to do so in an institution is a terrible waste of time and talent.

Whose time, whose talent? The parent's and the child's. Because the best school can only supplement what is done at home in terms of reinforcing a positive value system. Nobody has yet devised a method of teaching compassion, empathy, sensitivity, and understanding in a crowded classroom, and nobody will. The only way a parent can instill these values in children is by example in everyday life with them.

Who is most qualified to raise a woman's children? She is. What qualified her? Those parts of her which are unique to her. Every woman is a specialist in the area of raising her child —whether she knows it or not—because of her special background, interests, and heritage, which are hers to transmit to her children. The best schools, the most expensive lessons, do no good if later on a woman says, "I can't talk with my children, yet I've done everything for them."

In reality, she may have done very little of lasting import for them. For in going her own way, and in sending them theirs, she withholds her self—which she alone possesses—from her children.

How can a woman implement the philosophy of transmitting what is hers—and also theirs—to her children? How can she help them become sensitive to others and to the world around them? How can she encourage in them creativity and inventiveness? What can a woman do *with* small children?

"With" is the critical connecting link between the woman happy at home and her young children, for it is the "with" that frequently differentiates the woman who truly enjoys being home with her children from the woman who is dissatisfied there. It is the "with" that enables a woman to communicate the essence of her self—her innermost human qualities—to her children. It is the woman who somehow has not been lucky enough to learn the "with" who fixates at the custodial stage of child care, who believes that the physical care and feeding of children are what motherhood and familyhood are all about. A woman who holds these beliefs doesn't find it too difficult to go off to work, leaving her children in day-care or with sitters. Yet, actually, the physical care of normal healthy children is but a fraction of what goes into a really rich mother-child relationship.

The woman who learns the "with" of interacting with her children has the opportunity to communicate to them her own interests and feelings, her own sense of self and self-worth. One such woman is twenty-nine-year-old Emily Armon, who takes pleasure in communicating to her children the enjoyment she derives from creative activity. "When an activity has a really happy personal memory connected with it, the activity usually remains a pleasant experience. I have the most wonderful memories of cooking with my grandmother; she used to get up and bake the bread at four in the morning in the summertime, to get it done before it was too hot. I remember she taught me to sift and to do everything alongside her. I try to do the same thing with the children," Emily says, "but not at four in the morning!"

Emily describes her own parents as "educated people who believe in doing work with their hands as well as their minds. They've transmitted this to me, and I hope to pass it down to my children, as well. I learned woodworking from my father, knitting and sewing from my mother when I was really quite young. My mother let me use the machine by the time I was nine. I learned not only the skills they taught me, but more important, I have such wonderful associations with these learning experiences."

Emily has a definite sense of purpose with regard to being home with her children which she attributes to her mother who "set a wonderful example to me. She is bright; she's 'with it'; she's vital and involved; and she was at home with us when we were growing up.

"I have chosen to be at home, too," declares Emily. "I have seen too many times the consequences of what happens when a mother isn't at home. I really fear the kind of people who will be raised in a generation of day-care centers. With a large, diverse group, you just can't give that one-to-one attention that a mother can give at home."

Another woman who believes in the lasting value of interacting with her young children is Sally Gordon, who loves "communicating my own zest for life to our boys. I like to play in the leaves with them in the fall and build snowmen with them in winter. And sometimes in the summer, I'll say, 'C'mon, let's go get an ice cream cone' just for the fun of it. I think childhood is a time for spontaneity, for enjoying the moment, something most adults are too busy to do."

Sally feels she missed a great deal in not having her mother at home when she was growing up. "My mother had to work to help make ends meet. As children, my sister and I knew she preferred to be with us, that she didn't want to be away from the family, but that there was no choice. There is an essential difference between women who *must* work so the family can get by and those who do so because they really don't want to be at home, and this gets transmitted to the children early.

"Luckily, I can stay home with our two boys, and I view this as a luxury, even though two rowdy preschoolers can be enough to drive me nuts some days. Basically, what I do with them depends on what they're doing, which is usually a combination of imaginative and realistic play. And some of what we do together amounts to their coming with me on errands like the grocery store or the dry cleaners. This can either be a drag, or a lot of fun, depending on how you approach the whole thing. My approach is that these excursions are great adventures. We make shopping lists together and the boys help grocery shop. Each boy is responsible for getting certain things from the aisle into the basket. We have a lot of fun on these trips, and besides I think this is a good way for the boys to develop a sense of responsibility."

Anne Raydon enjoyed being home with her preschoolers so much that she chose to extend this phase of her life by having another child recently. "With Lisa in school all day, and Tommy in kindergarten, of all my options, I realized what I wanted most was another child. I think what I enjoy most about raising our children is watching them grow and develop in new ways each day. It gives me insight into their personalities and into my own, as well.

"When Lisa, our oldest, was born, I believed in the story about molding a child. That didn't last long. You don't mold a child, but you sure can guide him along the paths of his own abilities and interests. I enjoy being part of the development of the things that I feel matter most in a person—the sense of humor, the sensitivity."

Anne does with her children what she herself enjoys, passing on, by example, her enjoyment to her children. "I love the out-of-doors. Lisa and Tommy and I bike together a lot. Now Ro goes in a seat on the back of mine. We find bike-hikes a fun way to explore our surroundings, and a good outdoors kind of activity. Sometimes half the neighborhood joins us; sometimes it's just us.

"I've taught both Lisa and Tommy to swim, and Ro will probably be a fish, too, soon. We swim every day during the summertime, so she's already spent one summer in the water."

Anne says many of the things she does with Lisa and Lisa's friends could perfectly well be done without her. "I know it, and so do they. I don't come along as a supervisor, or a chaperone. I'm a companion to them, they're companions to me. Lately, we've started a creative dramatics group on Thursday afternoons for neighborhood kids. Sometimes there are fifteen grade-schoolers of varying ages; lately two or three of the other mothers have been coming, too.

"There aren't many mothers around our area during the day. A number of the kids in our area are 'key kids'—their moms are back in school or have gone off to earn another color TV. That's okay if that's what they want, but I really believe that it's unfair to impose too much responsibility on a child so young. Sure a first- or second-grader *can* come in and get his own cookies and milk, and he can find his bike and go play. But sometimes I think the child is putting up a bold front to the mother who says, 'You'll be fine, now, won't you?' Not wanting to disappoint her, he may say, 'Sure I will, Mom,' and he will be okay on the outside, but what about on the inside?

"My mother was always home with us; I have such happy memories of her being around after school when I came home, and I knew my friends were welcome, too. She was there to talk with us, if we wanted to talk. I want to provide our children with this same kind of security and communication."

It seems every woman I talked with used her own mother as her reference point. There were women like Sally Gordon, whose mother had to work to help pay for basic family living expenses and who themselves were happy for the opportunity to be at home with their own children. There were women like Emily Armon and Anne Raydon, whose happy homes, with mothers at home, prompted their decisions to be at home with their own children.

Like Emily and Anne, I was lucky enough to have a mother who was at home with my sister and me, doing things with us in our early years, just kind of there to talk with, later on. Because I had a happy childhood, quite naturally and without ever really talking with her about it, I assumed I would automatically be the kind of mother to our children that my mother has been to me.

Nonetheless, even with a very positive model, motherhood did not come easily or all at once. When I was first at home with a young child, twelve years ago, I felt out of place. I hadn't the faintest idea of what to do with a child, albeit a child we'd long planned and waited for. I'd never done baby-sitting, and my own mother didn't live nearby, where I could call her for advice or ideas.

That was 1964. Women's lib was starting to boom. Leaving home was legitimate and leaving home to return to a world of certainty—school or work—would surely have provided me with an easy way to avoid both the responsibilities and the joys of motherhood. Sitters were plentiful in Cambridge (day-care was not yet in vogue) and the atmosphere was highly charged with the excitement of intellectual accomplishment. There were all sorts of "neat," "exciting," "really stimulating" jobs around, or so I was always hearing from women who had them and were chronically searching for other mothers to take jobs, too, perhaps in part to justify their own positions.

But college and work had been full of easy answers—I guess I needed a challenge. Or maybe it's just that I'm stubborn and don't like to follow the crowd unless I'm sure *they're* sure where they're going and why. Perhaps it was the influence of Corine Street. But for whatever reason, I decided that although I felt unprepared to be at home with a child, home was exactly where I was going to be.

At the root of this decision was an analysis of the reason for my own idyllic childhood. My mother had been in a position similar to mine—away from school and her career—at home with a small child. Yet, she didn't leave me, and she didn't stay home and complain. She took long walks with me, we hiked in the woods, we had picnic lunches amid a carpet of purple violets. And she read to me—books by the dozens, by the hundreds. In spending time with me, in sharing simple activities with me, she communicated a great deal about herself, and her feelings about the world. This established not only a life-long bond of closeness, but also imbued me with a sense of security and happiness which I wanted to communicate to our own children.

I felt if I relaxed and enjoyed life with my daughter as my mother had with me, things would work out. They did, too, better than I ever dreamed. As our family grew, a whole new world opened; a world of re-experiencing again with children the everyday parts of life we as adults take for granted. Each of our three children has provided me with untold hours of enjoyment and each has added a new dimension to my life.

Miriam, who made me a mother, like most first children shouldered the responsibility of breaking me in. She showed me that I could have my sleep interrupted once or several times a night and survive, practically intact, through the next day. With her I re-experienced the joy and security of having a constant, loving, daily companion: I hadn't spent every day, day in and day out, year in and year out, with one person since my childhood days with my mother. Reading to Miriam, walking with her, talking with her, took me back to that very carefree time of my own life. What fun Miriam and I had wandering the streets of Cambridge, browsing in bookstores, adding to her book collection and mine, swinging in Fresh Pond Park, visiting with other mothers and children.

When Rachel was born, three years after Miriam, like most second children she fell into an ongoing way of life. She snuggled with Miriam and me when we read books, went where we pushed her by carriage and stroller, watched while we played, and one day got on her feet and joined in.

From then on my two junior colleagues and I had the best of times together, with Rachel no longer toted along, but rather a full participating member of our group. At that time, we returned to Minnesota, where wintertime meant sledding on the small hill in our back yard, and later, down the big hill at the corner. We'd become overwhelmed with laughter as we'd spill on top of one another, and red-cheeked with the cold as we refused to heed our numbing fingers and toes while one and then another of us insisted on "just one more slide." During the spring, summer, and fall, we'd eat our lunches outdoors, since food tastes so much better eaten among the dandelions. We'd often go "park-hopping," which meant using all the equipment in each of several parks, in one day. Sometimes we'd "do" three parks, picnicking at one of them, then top the day with a stop at the zoo. When we were indoors we three spent happy hours coloring, painting, and chalking together, taking great pride in the pictures we considered good enough to hang on the living room walls.

When Miriam began school, our trio was down one for part of each day, but Rachel and I made the best of it, and the most of it. Those were our "private years." We still sledded and read, filled the house with artwork and park-hopped, but in addition we got to know each other in a special way.

When it became evident that our days together were going to be intruded upon by the law of the land, it was time for Rebecca. She arrived in the nick of time, just a few months before Rachel left home—for morning kindergarten.

Rebecca, like most third children, came into a fully developed family, with experienced parents and competent older siblings, and thus seemed to mature immediately. Nonetheless, she and I have taken pleasure in doing all the things the "big girls" and I did together when they were younger, plus a few things of our own. Rebecca and I are a mobile mother and daughter, responsible for getting the older girls to school and back and delivered to their various activities. As long as Rebecca and I are out anyway, we shop and do errands together, frequently including a children's library or bakery stop on the way. We take walks along the Mississippi River banks and have running conversations with the cardinals, robins, squirrels, and caterpillars we encounter. Rebecca skated circles around me last winter, and this year claims she and I are starting on cross-country skis.

Next year when Rebecca begins school, my years in Phase One will come to a close. As I reflect on these years, I realize more than ever how lucky I've been to have had the economic opportunity to *choose* to stay at home with our girls—and how thankful I am that I took advantage of that opportunity.

BEING THERE AFTER SCHOOL

The importance of a woman's being at home when her children are there does not diminish when children are in school all day. "Being there" to greet and talk with their children when they come home from school is considered by many women a *must*. And understandably so. A child coming home from a day at school is often exuberant, and sometimes hostile. Some days there are happy tales to relate, other times small and occasionally big hurts. Who cares about these daily matters, these little things that go to make up a lifetime? Surely not a teacher busy with dozens of children, and certainly not peers who have their own ups and downs. (While exchanging confidences with peers is an important part of growing, often it's the peers who become the momentary problem: "Tracy isn't my best friend any more." "Billy likes Susan more than he likes me." "Judi and Paula have been whispering all day; they didn't let me play with them at all.")

Often one tends to forget how much it means to a child or a young person to know that somebody who cares will listen and comfort, or listen and laugh. A woman raising a family often underestimates the importance her role as listener-and-counselor plays in the ultimate development of the spirit of her children.

If a woman sits in an office behind a door marked "psychologist," "social worker," or "special interest counselor," with a stream of grade- and high-schoolers coming in and out, telling her what's on their minds and in their hearts, she might feel that what she is doing is more valid than sitting in the kitchen listening to her own children. After all, she'd have a job title and a paycheck—the earmarks, in today's terms, of personal validity. But what she said to the children she counseled would matter a great deal less in the long run. For in touching many lives briefly one bears less responsibility for each than when one devotes a great deal of time and psychic energy to a few who matter a great deal. Listening, day after day, responding when necessary and learning to keep quiet when necessary (an art in itself), may be the single greatest contribution any woman can make to the lives of her children. For communicating to them that she cares about them, about what they think, about what matters to them, is the only way that they will learn to care.

"What I feel is most important, now that the children are not little ones anymore, is that I'm available to listen and talk with them," says Gretchen Kingsley of her relationships with her three teen-age daughters and ten-year-old son. "Children thrive when they know their parents have genuine concern for them. I'm interested in everything each of our four does; children know when interest is sincere. One can't just say an absent-minded 'uh-huh' while doing something else; one has to really listen and respond to what she hears.

"One of the best times of day for talking is after school. Often when the girls come in from school we sit down, one of them puts the kettle on for tea—and we talk things over. This just seems to come naturally; I don't recall that we planned it in so many words. Alan doesn't sit, he bounces around the kitchen, in and out of the cookie jar a dozen times, or stands hands on hips in the doorway, listening, then bursting into the conversation with a joke or two. That's his way of being part of what's going on without admitting he really wants to be."

Alice Hastings, who has four school-age children, reports that after-school time is important in the lives of her family, too. "The older children start coming in at three; from then until four or four-thirty, I don't do anything but listen," Alice says. "I'm always at the kitchen table when they come home with plenty of snacks available, and we just talk. The afternoon snack time is as important as any meal for talking; everybody is happy and excited and fresh with news of the day. I wouldn't miss this time with them for the world!"

Marge Lafferty, who has three of her five children in school all day, also speaks of after-school time as important. "After three, the school kids start coming home. From then until dinner time it's hard telling how many people will be in and out of the house—talking and snacking. I never do any sewing during that part of the day," says Marge, who designs and sews evening wear—"Heavens, the red velvet would be full of orange juice stains and chocolate cake crumbs if I did."

Friends usually stream in after school with the Lafferty children. "There's so much going on around here, because of our sheer number, that I guess we just attract more," Marge laughs. "I like having our kids bring their friends in—that way I know where ours are and who they're with! I don't do anything special to court their coming. On the contrary, I often put them to work."

The Laffertys are in the midst of remodeling their suburban ranch-style home. "We're doing it all ourselves. Joe is an electrician, so he does much of the technical work, and I'm pretty good with a hammer. But there's plenty to be done by all willing hands. We're adding a large bedroom and also a big family room. So when the older kids and their friends are around in the afternoon, I often toss them some nails and say, 'C'mon, get to it!'"

Many women who are involved in personal activities during the hours their children are in school find it tempting to try to cram all sorts of chores, phone calls, errands, and even naps into after-school hours so that after school becomes a time either to be away from home or to be home but not available for talking with one's children. This is an easy trap to slip into, and bears watching, for it's the same kind of situation that the mother who works all day often faces—a harassed, not-quite-caught-up feeling that can envelop a woman so easily and prevent her feeling relaxed.

PRIVATE TIMES

Every child craves attention from, and interaction with, each parent; and conversely, each parent needs a personal relationship with each child. Regardless of how the recognition of these needs is implemented—whether a private time is a quiet conversation, a busy activity, or an errand turned special—it's essential that within the constellation of active family life, each parent finds a means of maintaining an individual relationship with each child. Those are the building blocks of future relationships, and so, too, the building blocks of successful total family life.

Different persons find different ways to implement this private time. "We've got diapers on one end, and cub scouts on the other, and we enjoy it all," says Angie Aselo, "but that means planning individual activities with each child; with four children, it takes organizing. It's well worth the effort, because both Nic and I feel it's important to keep up a one-to-one relationship with each of the children as they grow. When we had just the two boys, it wasn't really anything that required conscious effort; we just broke into twos from time to time and automatically found we had time with each child. But since the two girls were born, it's more complicated.

"On Saturdays, I alternate taking one child, then another, to the library to select books just for that child. It gives us some private time together, each child feels a sense of importance for being the only one going.

"We're two hours by train out of New York City and once a year I take each one of the older children down for the day with me. We go on a Saturday so Nic is with the others and usually plans a special kind of day at home for them. I love having the train ride each way alone with each child, taking him to museums, to lunch, and just looking around. The children look forward to their 'day in the city with Mom,' too. This is the stuff of which memories are made.

"Nic does individual things with the children mostly in the line of sports. He's a tennis whiz and at ten and eight the boys are getting pretty good. The girls are too young for tennis, though Nic thinks he'll have Jeanie on the courts by next year."

It's a long way from New Jersey to Nebraska but Angie and Nic Aselo and Alice and Steve Hastings have similar attitudes when it comes to making special time with each of their children.

"In the summertime," Alice says, "I take each of the school-age kids with me, one at a time, to Lincoln just shopping or looking around. Our town is small, less than five thousand, so I think it's good for the kids to just go somewhere else once in a while.

"Steve, too, makes time to take one or another of the children off with him, regularly. And at Christmas time, Steve does something really fun, I think. He takes each child out for lunch and shopping for gifts for everyone else. This is an outing which the children anticipate from October on every year."

Alice Hastings has developed an ingenious method of organizing her household so things get done, and she has time with each child in the process. "We have 'committees' set up for responsibilities around the house. The older four children are on kitchen committee and all it means is every fourth night he or she sets and clears the table and loads the dishwasher, with me. This accomplishes two things: the obvious, getting things ready and cleaned up, and more important to me, it ensures that I get a chance to talk with each of the school children individually every fourth night. Since nobody wants to get conscripted to work, nobody else comes near us. We got our dishwasher just last year; I'm almost sorry, because dishes used to take longer, and the washing and wiping activity meant even more individual after-supper time."

Gretchen Kingsley expresses the philosophy that "privates" are important in a slightly different way when she reflects: "Parents must sense when a child needs a little individual, extra attention, or when there's been a hurt. You must be tuned in." She arranges a private time—a shopping errand, a walk, a soda at the drugstore—whenever she feels a child needs or wants it. Her husband "often takes one or another to the library of an evening"—a simple, but important, recognition of the fact that each child needs individual time with each parent.

These one-to-one "privates" work both ways. Parents need them, too. I take each of our older girls out to lunch two or three times a year. Often this is preceded or followed by dentist or eye-doctor appointments, or school shopping. Yet the lunch together turns what could be a routine and not always pleasant chore into a happy event. This is a throwback to my own childhood when my mother used to take me to the eye doctor, then lunch and shopping while the eye drops took effect. I could never read the menu, nor see the prints and plaids all that clearly, but eye-doctor trips are very happy childhood memories. Mother and I were off by ourselves!

My father also used to take me out with him. He was an inveterate hiker; an after-dinner stroll to him was a four-mile round-trip walk into town to the drugstore. But, tired as I got, I loved it, as it provided time to talk with him about whatever was on my mind, and to hear stories of his youth in Hibbing, his beloved home-town on Minnesota's Iron Range.

My dad used to take me fishing, too. He liked to fish at sunrise, and some of the best times I can remember were spent out in a boat with him, at five in the morning. Although I wouldn't worm my own hook nor take the fish off, he took me along for companionship. He also liked to fish on sultry summer nights, and often took me with him to a spot where "they'll really bite," a rickety old bridge in mosquito-infested woods about twenty miles from our home. With layers of oil of citronella, long pants and a shirt down to my fingernails, and a large, floppy hat, all to keep my head, neck, and body protected from the insects, I went along, not to fish but to watch. Daddy enjoyed it so much that it was fun being with him, although the atmosphere left a lot to be desired!

I don't take our children fishing, but it isn't surprising that I consider an after-dinner walk, with one child, a natural way to have a "private" with her. It's fun to walk along in the dark talking about life in general and whatever specific part thereof is on the mind of my companion. I find this is a time to reminisce with each of them about my own childhood, just as my father did with me.

Dick enjoys "privates" with our daughters, too, and often turns an errand or quick trip to his office in the evening into a "private" with one of them. During the summer he gives each girl individual swimming lessons, in front of our rented lakeshore cabin, and plays tennis with each of them, at the neighborhood courts. (This includes almost 5-year-old Rebecca—"Wham-o"—who, since she "took up" tennis at three, has made up for in enthusiasm what she still lacks in co-ordination.)

Dick communicates his appreciation of music to the girls by spending special time with each of them at the piano, and listening with them to classical music. They have an ongoing game of "guess the composer," where one gets points for correct answers as well as credit for incorrect identification if she has figured out the right period and has good reasons for her choice.

Opera-going is another kind of "private" which Dick enjoys with each older girl. When he took Miriam to her first matinee at age eight, she found it love at first act. Since then, he's taken her every year when the Met comes to Minneapolis. She's now graduated to evening performances while he takes Rachel to the matinees. Dick considers himself a lucky man to have so many attentive dates; next year Rachel will also go evenings, and Rebecca will begin afternoons.

Each girl has been kept up for hours many a night by Dick's bedtime stories, which he "hears" from the mice who live in Mr. Fotheringbottom's fruit cellar. These stories, which delighted Miriam and Rachel in their day, now keep Rebecca enthralled. The "fruit cellars" have a long tradition, since they were originated by Dick's father, Grandpa Bill, when Dick was a little boy.

Many families—our family among them—find that it really doesn't matter what form a "private" takes; what does matter is that parent and child have time together to know and grow with one another.

9

The Family Life Cycle

One of the most delightful discoveries made by new parents is that the old adage, "two's company, three's a crowd," is a positive statement. Three is the start of a crowd, and a crowd means a new kind of fun because many activities, once shared by two, expand to become whole family activities. Initially, the most enjoyable kinds of family activities grow out of the interests of husband and wife. When Miriam was small, and still our only child, Dick and I did what we enjoyed—taking a walk, going out for an ice cream cone, singing at the piano—and Miriam was automatically a part of it.

But, as Miriam grew, we mistakenly designed some family outings specifically for her enjoyment. One of the most memorable of these occurred on a beautiful April Sunday afternoon, when Dick, Miriam, and I might have walked along the Charles River, had I not decided that Miriam needed a trip to the zoo. In fact, I maintained that since she'd already passed her second birthday, we'd deprived her in not having taken her sooner. No more time was to be lost, so we hastened through heavy traffic and arrived at the Boston Zoo to find that half the city's population had the same idea. Nonetheless, we doggedly made our way through the crowds, to all the cages, Miriam on Dick's shoulders so she could see the bears, tigers, lions, farm animals, and peacocks. We finally returned to the car, tired and irritable, and Dick and I felt worse when on the way home we asked Miriam what she'd seen at the zoo, and she sleepily re-plied, "lots and lots of people."

This incident points up a very important fact of family life: there is no sense in a couple's doing what they'd rather not do because they think it will be "good for the children." Invaria-bly, the result is good for nobody.

Children develop their own early tastes and interests through exposure and participation. Thus, when joint family activities are an outgrowth of what the couple really likes and wants to do, children grow up enjoying some of the same things their parents do (disliking other of those activities, and as they grow older, introducing their parents to yet new activities). It is im-portant to the total family constellation that from the earliest years each child be made to feel an integral part of the activi-ties of the whole family. In that way, both the individual and the family grow together.

The woman who believes that the family is the individual's basic support group feels a commitment to creating opportu-nities for members of the unit to enjoy as many conversations and activities together as possible. Women who share this sense of commitment agree that there are certain constant times which are necessary—each day, each week, each year—for es-tablishing and maintaining a secure, ongoing home life. These constants include family meals eaten together on a daily basis, joint activities at the end of each busy work week, vacations and traditions celebrated together during each year.

DINNERTIME/TALKING TIME

Usually the one time each day a family can count on spend-ing together is dinnertime. The main difference between a boardinghouse and a home is that in a home, dinnertime can be a time to sit down and relax, the meal being the event around which time for communication is built. In contrast, a succession of people parading into the kitchen filling their plates, gobbling their meal, and going off to whatever else they're doing does not constitute a pleasant, shared experience and is divisive, rather than supportive, of family life.

Often, even when people do sit down together, dinnertime is harassing, hectic, a period to get through as quickly as possible before other activities take over, rather than a time for leisurely conversation and laughter. One reason for this is that dinner is a time of transition in the daily cycle of most family members. It's a time when masks worn at the office, or with playmates, are cast aside and persons become most themselves. Thus, it's often a period for mass unwinding, and unwinding takes time; it can't be done in five minutes.

Women who strive to make the dinner atmosphere relaxed and leisurely say that it takes effort. Either meals have to be co-ordinated to fit into the varying schedules of members of the family, or else a firm time has to be established and held to. Once the goal of dinner as the time for the whole family to sit down and talk with one another in a relaxed way is defined, the particulars of timing are not impossible to work out.

"Dinner is our daily family time," Sue Robertson says. Whether the Robertsons are in the city or at their lakeside cabin, "we enjoy mealtime together. Every one of us—my husband Eric, the three boys, and I—is busy and involved in our interests, school activities, and community projects. But somehow none of those things manages to take precedence over our family life. Neither Eric nor I have ever said anyone *had* to be home for dinner, but we do discuss everybody's commitments for the day at breakfast, so that a convenient dinnertime is made available. It seems our boys just want to be where there's some good conversation, food, and fun, and that seems to be right here!"

Marge Lafferty also works to keep family dinner a regular daily activity. "I'd rather be flexible and have all or at least most of us here," says Marge. "Although my husband's job is predictable and I can always count on his being here well before six, the older kids are the ones who have different timetables. One has basketball practice this afternoon, another has choir practice that evening. We set up our dinnertime schedules for the week when we plan menus on Sunday nights. One night we may eat at five-thirty, another not until seven. The time doesn't matter; what does matter is that as many of us as possible eat dinner together."

MaryBeth Carlson values family "dinner" so much that she even moved it to 7:00 A.M. "You see," MaryBeth says, "for many years our family enjoyed a leisurely evening meal, but now that our children aren't such children, all four of them are in junior high and high school, busy with part-time jobs, and active in sports and school events, the schedules conflict so that we can't find a time that doesn't exclude somebody.

"We've solved the problem by having a big family dinner at breakfast time. I get up at six-thirty and have what has become our main meat meal of the day on the table by a little after seven, by which time everybody is dressed and ready. We sit around eating and talking until eight or so, then everybody is on their way. We've all agreed that it's worth trading a few minutes' sleep to begin the day in this way."

Families who value mealtime together often find as the children grow older and busier that they have to make sure to establish mealtime in one of two ways: either as the Carlsons have done, by having a firm time each day to which everyone fits his schedule, or by deciding every day as the Robertsons do, or every week as the Laffertys do, on the basis of the various activities of family members what time dinner will be.

WEEKENDS

The largest block of time, other than vacations, available for members of the family to be with one another is the weekend. Women who seek to make the weekend a real end to, and diversion from, the routine of the week, find each member of the family feels refreshed from the break in schedule it offers.

Some families use weekend time for family excursions, others for sharing a spectator or participant sport, still others for having friends join the family for meals or activities. In talking with various women about how their families utilize weekend time, I was frankly surprised at the many who spoke of their families going to church, or synagogue, as a natural part of their lives.

Apart from whatever its spiritual implications, it seems the religious institution itself serves a kind of double function in the lives of many families. First, it's a tie to other families and thus gives a sense of community, of belonging to a unit within the total social order. Secondly, it serves as a focal point around which other family activities are built. The family meal—Sunday dinner or brunch or Friday-night dinner—often precedes or follows a religious service.

"Our most special, most exciting, most favorite day of the week is Sunday," Alice Hastings says. "The older girls, Josie and Karen, both sing in the church choir on Sunday morning. The rest of us go to church together. After church we have our special meal of the week, in the dining room, with good china and silver."

Rebecca Edam speaks as enthusiastically about the celebration of her family's Sabbath. "Every Friday night, when the Sabbath begins, we have Sabbath dinner in the dining room. We begin at sundown by lighting candles and saying prayers; then we enjoy a long, leisurely meal followed by singing. On the Sabbaths when we invite other families, we dance afterwards, too. Saturday, we all go to synagogue services together, then have lunch and spend the afternoon either just resting or visiting with friends."

Making a special day out of their Sabbath, be it Saturday or Sunday, ensures a family that it has at least one day a week which isn't a workday, but which is special for family activities. It gives a break in the work-week routine, a time to wind down and relax individually and with others.

While some families chose to spend weekend time together quietly, others prefer joint outings and physical activities. Sue Robertson smiles happily as she speaks of her life with her husband, Eric, and their sons aged seven, eleven, and fourteen, "Our family loves to play together, and weekends serve our play purposes well. We skate all winter, and swim all summer. This is not unusual." What she feels is distinctive is that they build the play areas themselves. "Just as the preparation of any party is half the fun, building our skating rink every fall, and working on our cabin springs and summers, is, indeed, half the fun."

Every winter the Robertsons' large back yard is transformed into a skating rink. "As soon as it's cold enough, we all pitch in on weekends to build the frame, and flood the rink in preparation for a season of good fun. Then it's skating after school, hockey matches and skating parties every weekend. I couldn't begin to estimate how much hot chocolate we go through in a winter—but we once figured out that unless we use at least a hundred marshmallows a week something's wrong; either flu or an unseasonable thaw."

Sometimes the Robertsons' rink isn't even melted before they are off weekends to the cabin in Michigan, which, Sue says, "we're renovating ourselves. Actually, we renovated the main part of the eighty-year-old cabin three years ago, but there's always something left to do. Our main project now is an addition which we're building onto it. The kids have so many friends come that, even with lots of sleeping bags, we just don't have the room in the cabin as it now is."

Another family who takes advantage of weekends to provide them with time together are the Bradfords. Carol Bradford says she, John, and their children, recent transplants to Denver, "take short side trips, forty or fifty miles or so, on a weekend and acquaint ourselves and the children with the history and geography of the area. We just pack up a picnic and take off for the day; we often collect interesting rocks for the jewelry I make, and John always brings his camera. Knowing the area, perhaps as well or better than people who have grown up here, makes us feel like we really belong here now, too."

Like the Bradfords, we often spend weekend time enjoying the countryside in our home state of Minnesota. Since we returned to Minneapolis eight years ago, we've spent many weekends exploring the land around us. When Miriam and Rachel, now twelve and nine, were small, we took day trips, driving to the country in every direction, visiting farms, apple orchards, and old Indian ruins. We'd climb through an old mill, no longer in use but preserved as a historical site, one day; look for arrowheads, the next. We learned about dozens of varieties of apples at nearby orchards, and hiked along the banks of the Mississippi delighting ourselves with stories of escapades we might have were we to stow-away in one of the boats. We picnicked in woods filled with wild flowers, then drove through farm lands, fantasizing about giving up city life, buying a farm, and working the earth.

As the girls grew older, we often left the city for the weekend, and drove to northern Minnesota where we'd inspect abandoned iron mines, or roam the north shore of Lake Superior, watching ore boats, and hunting agates. And just when we thought we'd exhausted every area of the state, had explored every spot, picnicked in every park, we found we were to begin all over again. Because, since Rebecca's birth, try as we might to convince the older girls that we all ought to attempt some new weekend activities, their answer is always the same. "But, we've got to take 'Becka to a farm," " 'Becka needs to see cows and horses," or "We have to take 'Becka to Lake Superior, 'Becka has to see an ore boat. . . ." The fact of the matter is that Miriam and Rachel love these parts of their home territory as their father and I do; and thrive on being tour guides this time 'round.

VACATIONS

Not surprisingly, many women raising families believe family vacations are paramount to the family life cycle. Vacations are the only prolonged period of time during the year that the family has to take a break from the yearly routine, stop and look back at the previous year, and "refuel" for the year to come. Perhaps most importantly, a family vacation draws the family closer through a shared experience to be remembered throughout the years.

For some families, vacations represent an extension of the kinds of weekend activities they enjoy. For others, vacations are a time to go somewhere new, or to try something different. The kind of vacation a family chooses is not as important as that a family does vacation together as a means of enjoying one another in a different environment, without their usual school, job, and other daily schedules.

"I can't begin to describe how I look forward to our camper vacations," says Vivian Welles, who lives in a large Los Angeles home with her husband Gary, and their four sons, ages five to fifteen. "At home, each child has his own room and each of us in the family has many individual activities. It's so wonderful to put all that aside, condense ourselves into the camper, and take off."

The Welleses take two or three short trips each year and every second summer they travel by camper to their home state of Wisconsin, where they vacation at a resort with Vivian's parents. "My parents are getting older," Vivian says, "and they spend more and more time each year with us in our warm climate. But we like to come back to Wisconsin, too. When we do, we all stay at a resort where my folks can just enjoy the children without having any cooking or other responsibilities."

Rowena and Jack Bronde also use vacation time to acquaint their children with their own home state, and to visit with parents and grandparents. "Both my husband and I are from Colorado," Rowena says, "and our families are both there. Besides, we've skied practically since we walked. So these two factors combine to make us Colorado winter vacationers."

As soon as their children's school is out for the winter break, Rowena and Jack and their two sons fly from Cincinnati to Denver, where they spend Christmas with their families, and the following week at a ski resort. "It's a wonderful way to see our families, to enjoy the outdoors together, and to get some good exercise, besides. We always leave wishing we could stay a month longer. I guess that's the test of a good vacation."

Ruth and Dan Stammens and their three children also combine vacation time with visits to friends and relatives. Dan is a Chicago high school principal who spends over a month each summer driving around the United States vacationing with his family. At the time I talked with the Stammens, we had never taken our family on a cross-country car trip, and therefore I was particularly intrigued with learning about how they travel.

"I come from California, and Dan from New York," Ruth

says, "and we have friends and relatives living in almost every state. When we travel, it's usually with a visit to family as an ultimate destination. But we take plenty of time along the way. Sometimes we stop and spend a day or two with friends. Other times, if we hit a city where we'd planned only to stay overnight and then find some unexpected interests—an excellent museum, a rodeo in town—we stay longer.

"When we're not with family or friends, we stay in motels with pools. Since we vacation in the summer, we picnic almost all the time, which means meals are no big expense. We buy fruit, rolls, and milk for breakfast; fruit and cheese for lunch; and maybe have ice cream or a root beer mid-afternoon. We usually stop driving well before dinnertime so we can have a swim and look around for a while. Sometimes we eat dinner in a restaurant, but most times we buy some meat and vegetables and cook out on our portable grill.

"Dan and I share the driving and find traveling in this way very relaxing. For this one month a year our family is basically responsible only to ourselves and for ourselves. It gives each of us a refreshing break from the school-year routine, and most of all allows us time for new and varied experiences together."

Barbara Bordon also cites "shared experiences in different surroundings" as the reason her family enjoys vacationing together. Barbara, her husband Hank, and their growing family live in upstate New York and usually take camping vacations "no more than a few hours from home." According to Barbara, "Hank splits his vacation, and we take several short camping trips to various parts of the state and sometimes into Canada during the summer. We like being outdoors, away from it all, sharing with the children another, less mechanized way to live. Sleeping in tents and cooking over a campfire make us realize that we can have just as good a time as we do at home, with much less space, fewer material goods, and no TV."

We, too, frequently vacation in an outdoor setting within a few hours' drive of home. We have two favorite spots in northern Minnesota, in each of which we rent a housekeeping cabin and stay for a week or two at a time.

One of our favorite places is a hand-crafted log cabin in a

birch forest not far from the Canadian border. Our days there are filled with swimming, canoeing, hikes through the woods following animal tracks, and berry-picking in raspberry and blueberry thickets. At night we cook out and sing around the fire to Dick's guitar.

Our other favorite place is a cottage on Lake Superior where we're lulled to sleep by the sound of the waves, and are often awakened by crashing storms. For years, Rachel and I used to hide under the covers during such storms (with our now four-teen-year-old black Labrador, Mephisto, cowering under the bed) while Dick and the other girls watched the storm from the window and laughed at us. Gradually, Rachel and I, too, have come to appreciate the majesty of the thunder and light-ning on the fierce lake, to the point where we now look forward to the very worst weather.

We spend the rainy days which inevitably follow the storms, on the cottage's screen porch engaged in gin rummy tourna-ments, reading, storytelling, and waiting for the sun to shine. In good weather there's nothing we all enjoy more than rock climbing on the banks of Lake Superior by day, then roasting hot dogs and marshmallows on the lake shore as the sun sets.

Like many other families who treasure their vacation time, ours is precious to us as time to enjoy life with one another without the cares and routines of the "real world."

TRADITION

Encouraging the creation and celebration of traditions is a way in which a woman can enhance feelings of cohesion within the family, and provide a sense of identification with what has gone before. Linking the past with the present, giving new meaning to old events, and old meaning to new events, is the purpose the celebration of traditions fulfills in many families. Thus, traditions, in homes that value them, mean a lot more than a bird on Thanksgiving and a tree at Christmas. A family tradition can mean a family's interpretation or reinterpretation of an event, or the creation of a new event. Some traditions begin quite unexpectedly, others are occasions of long standing to which a family gives its special kind of interpretation.

"A tradition at our house," says Anne Raydon, "is anything that happens more than once. In fact, sometimes I think it's anything that happens at all. For instance, the Halloween when Lisa was three we made spice cupcakes with orange frosting, decorated with faces of raisins, currants, and cherries. The next Halloween as I was absently loading packages of candy bars to pass out at the door into our supermarket cart, Lisa asked, 'But what about making the cupcakes?' And so we did, and we have, every year since."

A tradition which has "just grown" at the Hastings, Alice says, "is our Sunday-night supper. After having our big meal at noon, and an afternoon of relaxing with family and friends, Sunday night is treat night. We pop popcorn, and make malts in the blender along with sandwiches of whatever anybody wants. I can't remember how or when this began. It seems we did it once or twice, everybody loved it, and it became a Hastings' tradition."

Sue and Eric Robertson are among the numerous families who, away from their own extended families, have established new family interpretations for age-old occasions. "It's become our tradition to share Christmas with many of our neighbors," Sue says. "The first year we came to the Chicago area, we got together with two other families on Christmas for caroling and exchanging gifts among the children. None of us had families nearby and we all felt nostalgic for the Christmas times we remembered, so being together helped the grownups and was fun for the children. I suppose the first year it was like group therapy for the adults in a way.

"But as we came to feel more at home here, Christmas in *this* home has seemed where it should be. Now, 'Christmas at the Robertsons'' is a tradition for many of our friends and neighbors. We gather here after church in the morning, have an informal buffet and a lot of singing, and exchange gifts among the children. We draw names for all the children who will be coming, then each child brings one gift for the child whose name he or she has. That way every child gets something, and there's no large expense for anybody.

"It's a warm, cozy Christmas, a meaningful one. Perhaps all the more so because it's a tradition that developed out of loneliness and now instead of feeling lonely we feel surrounded by people who mean a great deal to us. And to me that's a part of Christmas, and of life, really. Even though most of the families who were with us then have become close friends over the years, we always are sure to include anyone we've happened to meet who is brand-new here, even if we've hardly said more than 'hello.' That's part of the tradition, too!"

Some traditions come about through a particular interpretation of an established event—like the Robertsons' Christmas tradition; some traditions just sort of happen, like the Raydons' Halloween cupcakes, or the Hastingses' Sunday-night suppers; and then there are the occasions that are part of one's heritage.

In the mad rush to become part of the American melting pot, many immigrants left their traditions behind. Now, with pride in one's heritage popular again, even families who feel little association in their daily lives with a religious or ethnic group find great delight in reactivating special traditions which are their birthright. Other families strive to keep alive traditions which their families have preserved all along.

Nicolas Aselo is of Greek extraction; Angie is not. Yet they are equally interested in imbuing their children with a sense of pride and feeling of identity with their Greek heritage. "It's our tradition to celebrate two Easters, both the one I grew up knowing, and the Greek Easter, which comes at a different time," Angie says. "I've learned to cook lots of Greek dishes and really felt the fruits of my efforts were borne out recently when a friend of Nicolas' family from Greece had dinner with us and afterwards said he thought I must be Greek, too."

Rebecca Edam also realizes the value tradition has to the individual and to the total family life. "We celebrate all our Jewish festival days—Hanukah, Passover, Purim. Our family favorite is Succot. In the fall, we build a little wooden hut outdoors called a Succoh. All the neighbors come to help us decorate it with fresh fruits and vegetables, gourds and pumpkins. Then, we eat there during the eight-day festival of Succot. We have other families come for meals in the Succoh on one or two nights of the holiday; and on a weekend afternoon, we invite the whole neighborhood over for wine, honey cake, fruit, and nuts. It's such fun, I hate for the eight days to end.

"Our special observances add a whole dimension to our life," Rebecca says. "This makes our family feel conscious of a special identity which sets us apart from every other family around us. It's our family style."

Another woman who values her ethnic tradition is Irma Baldwin, who takes pride in her African heritage. "My husband and I try to give our children an appreciation of our heritage, through accurate historical accounts of what other blacks have done, and are doing. And also through our music, and in the kitchen. I make many traditional dishes which have come down to me from my great-grandmother, and probably from *her* great-grandmother. I'm teaching our three children—our girl *and* the two boys—to cook the same way."

One kind of tradition that transcends all racial and religious lines is a birthday celebration. Sometimes it's tempting to de-emphasize birthdays. But, as anyone who's ever been forgotten on a birthday knows, though growing older might be disconcerting, growing older without anyone even taking notice of it is worse!

Birthday celebrations for each member of the family are a part of the Kingsley family tradition. "Since the children were little," Gretchen Kingsley says, "we have always planned a birthday surprise for each of them. There is always a party, as they know there will be, but the surprise is what kind of cake, what kind of present, and just the general excitement of the birthday. Now, the children take over when Mel or I have a birthday and they plan the surprise for us. They shop for gifts—as if we really need gifts—but actually what they come up with is often touchingly individual. And they'll bake the cake and make the dinner."

Lee Barton solved what can be, for many families, a birthday problem and in so doing added some extra fun to their family's birthday celebrations. "I came to realize that when the time drew near for one child's birthday, often the others would grow morose, and sometimes downright cross," Lee says. "So, one winter afternoon we decided to have an "unbirthday party." It was nobody's birthday, but each child made a little gift for someone else in the family and at dinner, we had a cake and sat around singing. The unbirthday idea went on in slightly different form from that time on. Now, when it's one child's birthday, that child buys or makes a present for each of the other children. The birthday person does get presents on his or her special day; but so does every other child in the family."

Birthdays in our family are much-awaited events which take us through the long winter season. Mine comes first in January, Dick's is in February, Miriam's and Rachel's in March, and Rebecca's in April. We're hardly over one birthday before it's time to begin planning for another one. Handmade gifts take precedence in value over "store-boughten" ones, and homemade cards are the rule—nobody ever buys one. We have a birthday and holiday wall in the dining room, on which cards are hung, and a birthday box, decorated by the girls, in which presents are secreted. Weeks before the actual event, there are long conferences, from which the birthday person is omitted, regarding the menu for the birthday dinner, a meal built around the favorite foods of the birthday person. (Birthday dinners at our house range from chocolate everything to *coq au vin*.)

At the dinner table on the children's birthdays we tell the Story of How It Began, "It" being the birthday person. Each girl delights in hearing her own story retold: how once there was no Miriam (or Rachel or Rebecca), then the mad dash to the hospital, and the thrill of the new member added to our family.

In addition to the traditional family celebration, the girls each have a party for their school and neighborhood friends. Although Miriam and Rachel attend parties with a wide variety of themes—costume parties and hobo parties, movie parties, bowling and roller-skating parties, slumber parties and camp-out parties, they each have their own traditional kind of party from which they never vary. That is a lunch at our house followed by a treasure hunt at the nearby University of Minnesota campus. The guests divide into several competing teams and are quite a sight to students passing by, as they search the premises for the treasure. As the girls grow older, Dick, who takes charge of this aspect of the party, finds designing the clues to keep the guests mentally challenged and physically active no mean feat. Last year's final clue, "Look for me on a symbol of peace," had everyone stymied for over an hour. Finally one team found the treasure—tied to an olive branch!

No family can have too many traditions. Regardless of how a family tradition comes about, and how it is implemented, in our nuclear age we're more than ever in need of feeling the security which the celebration of traditions affords us. "How come you like having the same kind of birthday party every year, and celebrating all the holidays in the same way all the time?" I asked Rachel some years ago. "Because it's fun and things come out the way I expect," she told me. Her reason is a sound one. In a world where so many things don't come out as we expect, it's reassuring to know that within one's family there are traditions which can be celebrated in the anticipated way.

10

Extending the Family

The woman who includes others outside the family group into family activities recognizes that the immediate family unit is strengthened by a support group which reinforces its values. She realizes that the formation of an old-fashioned kind of family life, where others come in and out of the home, freely and comfortably, is not only possible in the midst of the modern world, but that the need for a family's extending itself is more essential today than it has ever been.

Where a woman seeks to create an "open family" life, often much more than just hospitality is involved. Or, perhaps more accurately, a real old-fashioned kind of hospitality *is* involved, rather than the perfunctory politeness which characterizes so much formal socializing today. When a family includes others into its fold, for a meal, an activity, a day, there's a double benefit: a feeling of warmth and belonging extended by the family toward others, and equally important, the feeling of necessity and belonging received by the family. The close-knit extended family of yesterday is weakened or gone now. Though some say good riddance while others mourn it, what has not been extinguished among those who opt for family life is the need to feel one's immediate family is part of a community.

When one walks into a home where the members of the family really want to be, chances are that others outside the immediate family will be there too—school friends of the children, or neighbors, perhaps a young college student away from home, an older person or two, or another whole family.

Many families feel the importance of "linking themselves up" to others for a greater sense of getting and of giving a feeling of community. This philosophy is often expressed in a simple joint activity with other families—a meal, a sporting event, an outdoor concert, or a play.

Different families implement joint activity according to the interests of members of each group. Sally Gordon's family enjoys having another family or two join them for supper and a song fest. "After dinner everyone pitches in quickly to clean up, then we gather around the piano and sing. Lately, we've added a guitar to our family and sometimes it's the guitar instead of the piano, occasionally both. This kind of activity suits our life style as we have friends in various age groups. And music is a great common denominator; toddlers, teen-agers, and grandparents can all join in."

Lee Barton and her family frequently enjoy spontaneous get-togethers with other families. "For instance, one rainy Sunday afternoon recently we called two other families and asked them to come over and join us for games and a picnic in front of the fire. There were fifteen of us in all, ranging in age from two to forty. Some of us played bridge—the teen-agers are learning—others played Monopoly, and still others built clay railroads, farms, and castles. At the end of the afternoon I put out cold cuts and everybody made their own sandwiches and drank mugs of hot soup. Our family was going to stay indoors, play Monopoly, and have a sandwich supper anyway, so it seemed like a fun idea to make a party of it."

Kathy Jacovi's family particularly enjoys outdoor get-togethers with other families. "We have spent many a summer afternoon playing kickball with friends, having lemonade and hamburgers in their yard or ours, then finishing off the day with a game of croquet. Other times, we have another family over for a badminton game followed by ice cream sundaes. And in the winter, tobogganing together, topped off by cocoa or hot cider, is one of our family's favorite ways of having fun with friends," Kathy continues. "Tobogganing is a good mixer and it takes no training or talent and very little equipment. All you need is snow, a toboggan or two, and, of course, a hill."

Anne Raydon feels it's important to her and to her family to have other families around them. "I don't enjoy formal entertaining, so I've found brunch on Sundays a perfect time to have other families with us, on an informal basis. It's a fun and easy meal to make, particularly in the nice weather when we have picnic brunches in our back yard.

Marge Lafferty also finds brunch an easy time to incorporate friends into their family sphere. "We go to church as a family on Sunday mornings and then come home for a huge brunch, which the whole family helps to prepare. It's replaced the traditional Sunday dinner at our house. Our Sunday brunch-time is very informal, served buffet style, and is known to our friends as open house time, so often we have a real crowd. Sometimes friends come right on home from church with us; other times, they come over later on. Sometimes the kids drift outdoors and play, the teens congregate in the rec room, and the grownups may watch a football game, or just talk. Other times, we all go out and play a 'mixed-generation game,' like softball, or in bad weather we have a series of card games going."

Another kind of occasion that encourages a feeling of closeness to develop among families is a pot-luck supper, lunch, or brunch, where every family brings part of the meal. "We particularly enjoy pot-luck get-togethers to welcome new families to the neighborhood," Emily Armon says. "Then several families divide up a menu, nobody has much work, and everybody can have a good time. Space is the only problem. Sometimes you wonder how everyone is going to fit—after all, six families can mean twenty-five or thirty people, but somehow we've had our best times in what seemed the most cramped quarters."

We've had good times in a tiny apartment filled with the laughter of people of all ages, and in the smallest of homes. It's the attitude that counts, not the space. And unless someone's got back trouble, what's wrong with sitting on the floor?

TO ELDERS

One way families extend themselves is by sharing activities with other families; another way is by including persons of various ages and circumstances into the family's activities.

"Because we're transplants, we've tried, since we've been settled in Denver, to make friends among persons of different age groups," Carol Bradford says. "It adds another dimension to our lives. We are quite close to Sal and Carl Pederson, who are about the age of my own parents, who live in New Jersey. The Pedersons invite us over on a Sunday from time to time, or we invite them to be with us when it's a holiday or one of the children's birthdays. They are parent and grandparent surrogates, no doubt about it. And since their family is grown and lives away from Denver, we are child and grandchild substitutes to them."

Margo Reiter has made it a point to develop friendships with several older persons and make them a close part of her family's life. One friend is Mrs. Marling, a widow from whom Margo and her husband bought their home three years ago. When Mrs. Marling sold it to them she reminisced about all the happy holidays her family had spent there when her husband was alive, and her children were near. Margo responded immediately, "You'll spend every holiday right here with us in your own home!" And Mrs. Marling has. She's provided Margo's family with the feeling that there's a grandmother in the house, and Margo's family gives her the feeling that her family is somehow still there. Mrs. Marling invites the Reiters to a meal in her apartment some Sundays, and frequently takes one of the Reiter children on an outing, for lunch or to a movie.

Just about all of us know someone who is alone like Mrs. Marling. Or we know couples whose grown children and grandchildren live away from them. Yet we're often so used to making friendships only among persons of our own ages that we don't think about inviting those older than we to join in our family lives. So we miss out and they do, too. When one meets someone who is living alone, or a couple whose children are not living near them, asking them to share in a family gathering can lead to enriching experiences for everyone involved.

Sometimes, the younger person feels awkward taking the initiative with the older ones, especially if the older persons have lived in the community longer. Before the mobile society, it was customary that the resident of longest standing "paid a call on" or "issued an invitation to" the newcomer. But this kind of formality is largely gone now (except from work-related situations . . . one still doesn't usually invite someone higher in the status hierarchy first, for fear of being thought to seek favor rather than friendship). When persons meet in the neighborhood, or socially, or through any kind of association except where one works directly under the other, it doesn't matter who takes the initiative; what does matter is that someone does. An older person is often flattered to be invited to join younger ones. Sometimes persons whose children are grown and gone come to feel as if they have, through no fault of their own, been forced into a generation gap. They are left with friends who are, like themselves, without children and grandchildren nearby, or worse yet, with friends who have their own children nearby and therefore who seem much more "with it." Persons whose families are grown and have moved away are frequently delighted when younger people seek them out, and they respond wholeheartedly.

SEEKING OUT ONE'S OWN EXTENDED FAMILY

Some persons with grown children are fortunate enough to have them living nearby and the grown children and grandchildren are lucky to be part of an extended family. Sometimes this geographical proximity comes about accidentally, and other times by design. The mobility craze, wherein the size of the man's salary and the length of his title have been the prime mover of families for the past several decades, is declining. Now, more and more couples beginning their families are looking at location as a major factor in their total life-style decisions. Frequently, the whereabouts of extended family is a vital aspect of that decision.

Stella Lingston and her husband Douglas, both raised in Akron, Ohio, and educated at Ivy League colleges, spent many months making a life-style decision as Douglas neared law school graduation. "Doug was Law Review, and an all-around outstanding student," Stella says, "so it wasn't surprising that he received attractive offers right and left.

"However, our son was then ten months old, and when it came right down to where we wanted to live and to raise him, we decided he and we would benefit most from living right in our own home town. Both Doug and I wanted to be where our parents, brothers, and sisters were, and where our children could grow up among them. Six years, and two children later, it has worked out beautifully. Doug is happy professionally, and we're all happy personally. I guess we're people who believe blood is thicker than water, and for us, anyway, it is."

In our own case, when an excellent job was offered to Dick at the University of Minnesota, we were thrilled to return to Minnesota, where our families live. Nonetheless, friends in Boston were surprised at our decision to leave the mecca of academe. "Someday your parents will be gone, and then you'll be left out there with all that snow," we were cautioned by one well-meaning friend anxious that we remain in Boston. I suppose that was one way to look at it. But we've never regretted our decision to seek out our extended family, to spend time with them in our adult lives, and to raise our children with the wonderful sense of security that a close extended family can provide.

One of the greatest all-around advantages of an extended family is that it's multi-generational, whereas in the world outside the family persons are structured into activities with age peers beginning with nursery schools and ending, never. (Witness homes for the elderly throughout the country.) Yet there isn't a family situation where age really much matters. We and our girls have wonderful memories of sitting around the dinner table, singing, when Rebecca was two and Grandma Bess was ninety-four.

At Grandpa Bill and Grandma Ruth's the younger children often stage a play, in which the elder two generations are invited to participate—occasionally as cast members, always with sets and costumes. When Grandpa Bill sits at the kitchen table with the girls—amid wax paper, knives, and huge orange pumpkins—at their annual pumpkin-design-and-carving fest, it's hard to tell whether he or they enjoy it most.

Our girls clamor to go to their Great-Aunt Minnie's, where she has "the best cookies," where Great-Auntie Ro gives impromptu instruction in crocheting and needlepoint, and where Great-Uncle John can be induced to tell stories of his young adulthood in northern Minnesota when nose-to-nose meetings with wild bear were quite ordinary occurrences. It's a special bonus when cousins Alan and Judy are there, too, as Alan is immediately pulled into a card game with one of the girls, while the others take turns having Judy fix their hair.

Although my father died two years ago, he is and will continue to be an everyday part of our thoughts and conversations, because he and we were an everyday part of one another's lives. We saw him often and he used to telephone each girl daily with a special message—for Miriam and Rachel it often concerned an upcoming television special, or plans for a movie they were all to see the following weekend; for Rebecca, the communication would revolve around what kind of candy she wanted to eat next, or he and she would concoct a new rhyme.

Similarly, we and the girls enjoy a close relationship with my mother. We all have dinner together frequently; Mother, Rebecca, and I do errands together, and we talk by phone a couple of times a day. The older girls take turns staying overnight with Mother during school vacations, each enjoying a "private" with her; and each returning from her stay with shining eyes, newly shampooed hair, and freshly manicured nails. The girls telephone Mother frequently with news of their school activities and occasionally with requests that she tell *her* daughter to let them stay out later or up longer.

AND THOSE YOUNGER

Not only is it important for persons to keep in touch with those who are older than they, but also with those who are younger.

Where couples have at least some of their grown children living in the same geographical area, keeping close to them and to their ideas needn't be a problem. That is, if the parents are wise enough to treat their sons-in-law and daughters-in-law just as they do their own children. According to some women, doing so is not always easy, but is well worth the effort.

Molly Blandon has a married son and married daughter both living in Los Angeles, each within an hour's drive of her home. "Frankly, although I like my son-in-law very much, it took me a long time to accept my daughter-in-law," Molly says. "She's very different than the other girls my son dated and I had a hard time warming up to her. But I realized that if I didn't treat her like a daughter I would very likely lose a son. So, I just made it a point not to give sidelong glances at the table when I thought she was out of line, and not to argue with her when she was determined she was right. Pretty soon, I didn't have to try so hard any more. She kind of grew on me.

"In fact when I was rushed to the hospital for emergency surgery a couple of years ago, my own daughter and her family were out of town. It was my daughter-in-law who came and took care of me the first few days back home. She's all right after all. It just took some knowing. Sunday is our family day when she, my son, and their family come for dinner along with my daughter, her husband, and her children. Sometimes they bring friends along with them, too. That's fine with us; we like keeping up with younger ideas even though we don't agree with them all the time."

Roma Flagley has grown children, and she, too, has found a means of keeping in touch with the generation younger than her own. "All three of our children are married and live out of town," Roma says. "On my husband's vacation we go and make the rounds visiting them. But, it's not like having them around the corner.

"To try and compensate for it, I guess, I started making friends among some of the new young couples that move into our area. A large corporation was built not far from us about ten years ago, and a lot of young executives and engineers and their families move in and out of here. Some of them are very lonesome, as most of them have not put down any roots yet.

"So, I invite some of the young women over for coffee, and do some grandmothering of their children; and we invite them for Thanksgiving and times like that. It fills a need for us, and also for them. We've made some wonderful friends that way."

Those of us raising growing families need to have friends among younger people, too. Otherwise, what often happens is that when we are somewhere between age twenty-five to thirty-five we begin to feel apart from younger people. Teen-agers seem so young; even college students seem in a different world. "We," through "their" perceptions of us, become Establishment, whatever that means. (It usually means we own houses, cars; have jobs.) And thus, we feel we've lost contact on the one hand with those older than ourselves and, on the other, with those younger.

By doing this we lose perspective on the fact that we're part of a continuum and tend, instead, to think of our particular age as an Age. Unless we maintain contact with both our elders and with those younger than we are, we don't learn much, firsthand, about what's gone on before us; nor do we learn about what's going on now. Then all of a sudden when our children reach their teens we're in a state of shock. We can't seem to talk with them because it's been twenty years or more since we've been teen-agers ourselves, and thus almost that long since we've had occasion really to talk with a teen-ager. Clearly the best way to avoid this form of culture shock is to keep talking with children, with teen-agers, with college students, and young working people.

If one wants to build friendships with younger persons, it isn't difficult to meet them, for it isn't only the little family unit that is alone today. Students go far from their own homes to college, and young working adults have moved far from their parents; thus, in every community—large or small—there are people of varying ages who are removed from their own close family relationships and might welcome a feeling of belonging to another family.

Most college students appreciate knowing they have a home away from home where they can come for Sunday dinner, or can drop in between classes. We've made many friends among students in various university settings. As they graduate and take jobs, they continue to keep us abreast of thoughts and feelings of young adults outside the university communities, too.

Many of these friends developed very close relationships with one or more of our children. Raleigh had our older girls as flower girls at her wedding, and each wore a dress Raleigh had made for them herself. Bob taught Rachel to pump herself on a swing when she was barely two and to ride a trike when she could hardly walk. He'd had several younger brothers and sisters at home, was accustomed to small children, and liked a chance to spend time with them. Hillary sends cards and letters from wherever on the globe she happens to be, and three years ago she made the girls a papier-mâché piñata, which they so cherish that it still hangs in their bedroom—fully intact.

Each of these friendships has been a mutually beneficial situation for us, for our girls, and for the students. Each has provided us with a bridge over the generation gap—because we have friends in their late teens and early twenties, older than our children, younger than we are. The students have found a substitute family situation, a place to go where somebody is interested in them, in their ideas and problems—where there's somebody to play with in one room, somebody to talk to in another, and a family with whom to share a meal or a holiday.

There are junior colleges, colleges, universities, and trade schools in many communities where not only American students away from their own homes are enrolled, but foreign students as well. If one wishes to meet some of them, all that need be done to get started is to call a dorm counselor, saying one or

two students, who are away from home, are invited for Thanksgiving or for a Sunday dinner.

KNOWING WHERE THEY ARE AND WHO THEY'RE WITH

Though it's often hard to realize, the most important people
to whom a family ever extends its hospitality are the children's
friends. Such hospitality doesn't always come easily. Toddlers
and preschoolers can be the messiest creatures alive; it's tempting to relegate them to the basement—preferably with a separate entrance and exit—or better yet, the back yard. Grade-
schoolers are perhaps less troublesome, but even two or three
extra in the house after school—in addition to one's own—can
seem like an invasion from outer space as they drop coats,
scarves, and schoolbags indiscriminately and make crumbs of
what might have been dessert for a couple of dinners. Teen-
agers are, of course, impossible to have around. They demand
utter privacy one minute, take over the house the next. They
whisper, they shriek, they play the stereo at ear-splitting levels,
and they gobble all that's in sight.

That's one way to view the situation. If so, it's sure that from
a very early age children will find it's more comfortable to be
with their friends elsewhere; perhaps in their friends' homes, instead. But if those families aren't receptive either, then where?
Unsupervised houses, where the parents are gone all the time
so nobody knows or cares if children and their friends are
around? Street corners? Where?

Women who are aware of the negative alternatives feel that
keeping home a positive, pleasant, welcoming place for children and their friends is of prime importance. Marge Lafferty
says, "I prefer to have the kids and their friends around here.
That way I know where our kids are and who they're with."

Not only was that precisely my mother's philosophy when we
were growing up, but those were her very words. Why, her
friends would ask her, did she put up with a living room full of
eleven-year-olds, a basement filled with fourteen- and fifteen-
year-olds, one minute dancing, the next playing ping-pong, the
next making milkshakes in what was probably the first blender

on the market. Why did she not object to the front porch decked with teen-age girls, feigning deep conversations while waiting for the boys to pass by on the way home from football practice? I sometimes wondered myself. We were noisy, we were messy, we were a constant invasion of adult privacy. Sue's house was never available; her mother entertained several times a week, and it had to remain neat and clean. Sandy's house wasn't open to us either; her mother didn't like the noise. Now, there isn't a person around who values cleanliness and order, peace and quiet, more than my mother. Nonetheless, she was terrific with our friends. Although she was involved in her own activities, she was available to talk with us when sought out, either by a group or individuals.

"Why do you always let us have the kids to our house, Mother?" I'd ask her. Mother would just smile and say, "I like it this way. I know where you are and who you're with."

My father liked having our friends around, too. He knew everybody's name and their current interest—quite a feat when various friends brought various new friends all the time, and interests changed by the day if not the minute! My friends from grade school still speak gleefully of the sleigh-ride parties he used to supervise for my birthdays. (Traditional division of labor: my mother stayed home where it was warm preparing the cocoa and food; my dad came on the sleigh in −20°.)

My parents' attitude that our friends were important people, worthy of the best of hospitality, time, and interest, is as valuable today as it was a generation ago. For there comes a time when the peer group exerts tremendous influence on the child. It's important for a parent to know who their children's peers are, and make them welcome, for two reasons. First, to provide reinforcement of values in the cases where children's friends come from homes with similar values. And second, to provide a positive example to children who may not come from homes where basic human relationships are valued. In setting a tone for what a warm, secure kind of atmosphere can mean and in welcoming one's children's friends—both those who come from homes with like values and those who don't—it's possible to influence the peer group, which influences one's own children.

Children who come from secure homes where human relationships are highly valued, not surprisingly, develop a feeling for places which "seem like home." They seek to spend time in their own home and in homes of friends with similar values. Thus, homes where the parents are rarely there, or are there but disinterested in the children and their friends, where there is little or no supervision, don't look glamorous. They look lonely.

Establishing guidelines for behavior—through example in one's own home—is the best and only insurance available that as children mature, they will adopt modes of behavior which are healthy for them, and are functional and helpful—rather than dysfunctional and disruptive—to the community.

11

Success of the Human Ethic

Among couples who place a high priority on their home lives, most often the woman arrives at this priority before her husband. With good reason. A man, raised in the success-ethic milieu, has no respite from it as he goes from college into a career niche. A woman has the opportunity to break out of the success-ethic pattern, to stay at home and raise her family, to do her own thing in her own time in her own way—to develop a human ethic.

Thus, where a woman values a warm, close family life, part of implementing these values within her home entails her being definite about her feelings toward her husband spending time with the family. Men are frequently not raised to expect to spend time with wives and children. They are often not brought up to expect to be wanted and loved for the human qualities they possess, but rather, are raised to expect to *support* a family. (And, while they're at it, to do it in as high a style as possible. The way to get ahead is to be a doctor, a lawyer, a merchant, a chief. To Be a Something. Serving as an ordinary meal ticket is hardly a fulfilling goal for the intelligent, able man; the success ethic dictates that such a man should instead aspire to be a high-class meal ticket.)

After the depression years of the thirties, breadwinning for the sake of feeding his family was not a lofty enough goal for many business and professional men; success became the greater goal.

Then, with the educational and economic inflation following World War II, the pursuit of success boomeranged into a full-time occupation. Personal fulfillment was "in," and the way to fulfill oneself personally was to succeed, through earnings and status. Success meant not only money enough to feed, clothe, and house a family but to do it in a style previously unknown except among a very few. Success meant spacious, well-furnished houses, a couple of cars, expensive vacations, good schools for the children; and it meant working long hours, evenings, weekends, and frequent traveling away from home to achieve it.

While the job orientation promulgated by this success ethic meant mobility and the disruption of extended families, it meant disruption of the resultant nuclear family unit as well. For while fathers worked long hours away from home, mothers stayed there, alone, caring for the children.

By the early sixties, family life experts concluded that women shouldn't be alone with their children so much. But the point that escaped many well-intentioned social commentators was that the problem was not an overdose of mothers but an absence of fathers. With the rise of the Mobile Society, with extended-family ties weakened or severed, the need for a husband and father—one who was both emotionally *and* physically present—was greater than it had ever been before. But where was he? At the office. And why not?

The office is the natural habitat for a product of social conditioning who grows up thinking in terms of how he'll make and spend money for his family rather than how he'll make and spend time with them.

Men have traditionally not been brought up to expect to transmit their own interests and passions in life to their children, but instead to expect that doing a good job outside home can mean more money to bring home, and also more status in which the whole family can revel. Thus, the absentee father is often not a selfish, self-seeking individual, but rather a "good boy" accepting the role his parents, teachers, and whole social order have imposed upon him. While he's busy being a "good boy," his wife and children, the very persons who are potentially closest in his life, frequently see him very little.

Since "family" almost always comes chronologically after a man has made a career choice, when the first child is born the father is either embroiled in schooling to lead to the ultimate function he'll perform, or is already performing it. "Family" is fit into his work habits, frequently haphazardly. Since family comes last chronologically—after the career choice and often after the career has begun—family also comes last in his everyday time allocations.

By the time a man is in his late twenties or early thirties, he frequently finds he's locked into a life style which gives him little time for either wife, children, or personal interests outside the immediate sphere of his work. A typical picture is that of a young husband and father working long hours and commuting fifteen minutes to an hour or more to his home. In the habit of taking his function wherever he goes, he usually brings work home. Whether he's a doctor, lawyer, engineer, professor, or businessman, his situation is essentially the same: he has established a way of life which presupposes that his function in life is his reason for being. With that function comes the life style his function buys for the family, the house and all its accouterments, its location, church and club affiliations, schooling and lessons for the children.

And what are the reactions of women "widowed" by a man's function, left alone to raise their children?

Some women, martyrlike, give their tacit approval, and in so doing, help—like Friedan's women of the sixties—to perpetuate the success ethic. They assume that in order to "fulfill" himself, a man has to work hard, and they equate working hard with working long hours, at night and on weekends, with frequent business trips or conventions, with dinner and evening meetings. In trying to be dutiful "corporation wives," "doctors' wives," "lawyers' wives," they not only accept that their husbands are what their functions are, but accept the reflection of that definition for themselves as well.

Other women resent the long hours and high dedication to

career which excludes family, yet they like the money and status of their husband's job. Still others pursue the success ethic themselves. Instead of raising their children, they raise consciousness, take jobs, and pursue careers outside of home.

There are, fortunately, many women who choose neither to accept passively the norm of the absentee husband and father, nor to imitate him by becoming absentee mothers. These women go beyond the success ethic to achieve a human ethic wherein home life is the number-one priority on the *joint* scale of family values.

These are women, some of whom we've discussed in preceding chapters, who themselves opt to be at home, who have encouraged their husbands to define with them the kind of family lives they build. As women who have found home a free and flexible base of operation, they encourage their husbands to be an integral part of the ongoing home and family life rather than just to pay for it.

Rebecca Edam has communicated to her husband that she values time with him, and time he can spend with the whole family, more than extra money he might earn during that time. "Rebecca's the one who says, 'Who needs it, I'd rather see you,' when I mention a project that would take time away from home, but will also bring in more money," Sam Edam says. "She's the one who pushed moving from a suburb into Baltimore so we could have more family time."

John Bradford, a Denver architect, values time with his family above "the more and more quantity of goods, less and less quality of life" existence he sees around him. John credits his wife Carol with encouraging him in this way. "I cut out working Saturdays so I could enjoy a two-day weekend, and I rarely if ever work at night any more. I started out in a large firm, working literally day and night. Carol and I hardly saw each other. It seemed the kids would grow up not knowing me very well, nor I them. So I hung it up, went into a smaller, lower-pressure office, and I have had no regrets.

"However," John says, "I would not have made that decision without Carol's continual encouragement. If I'd been married to a woman who thrived on the glory generated by the high-pressure job—we had some of the area's top clients, who frequently entertained us, it was definitely a high-prestige firm—and who loved to spend money, then I'd still be grinding away."

Eric Robertson says his wife Sue is responsible for his having quit "the transfer circuit" to settle on a position which allows him time with his family and for his hobbies.

"Until eight years ago," Eric remembers, "I was moving fast on the circuit. While job-wise it was gratifying to know that I was going places, unhappily it meant the whole family was going more places than we wanted; Los Angeles for eighteen months, then a short stint in Pittsburgh, out to Tacoma, then the transfer to Chicago.

"Each of our kids was born in a different city. Every time we got settled and hung pictures, we moved again. Sue was unhappy and lonely and rightly so. I was satisfied in the office, but I didn't have a home life.

"After thrashing it out over and over again, we came to realize that I was living almost like a bachelor and Sue was the next thing to a widow. The kids were pretty nearly in a fatherless home. I finally had to choose between my personal life and my corporate life. Once I realized that's what I had to do, I didn't hesitate. I told the powers that be that I wasn't in the market for another transfer; that we were happy with our setup here in Chicago, and we wanted to put down some roots. If they wanted me to leave the company, fine. If they felt there was a future in this branch of the corporation, I'd stay.

"They asked me to stay. I'm in a position which I enjoy and which is not draining me of all my time and energy. I'm able to be with Sue and the kids, whom fortunately I have gotten to know. I shudder to think what would have happened if I had stayed on the circuit for another five years.

"Without Sue's help, I would not have made this decision. She knew there would be substantial material loss involved, and also that she wouldn't be the wife of a company bigwig, unless we kept moving. But she didn't care; she preferred having a family life which includes me."

Sam Edam, John Bradford, and Eric Robertson are among a number of men who attribute their opportunities of spending time with their families to encouragement by their wives. For in families where home is the high-priority place to be, one hears again and again, "My wife really was the most important influence in my decision to work less, be home more. . . ." "Without my wife, I couldn't have done it. . . ."

More and more women and men are recognizing the absurdity of the success ethic which dictates that the family life must conform to the job, and instead are searching for ways of using their particular training, specialties, and skills to make jobs conform to their preferred life styles.

Mark Kramer, a highly successful attorney (where success is measured in terms of dollars earned, and titles accumulated) in a prestigious law firm, recently told me of the differences he sees between young men coming into his firm now as compared to those who began, when he did, in the mid-fifties: "All we thought about was moving ahead. We assumed that part of the game was taking work home every night, working all day Saturday, bringing work home for Sunday, and traveling where we were sent by higher-ups in the firm. We also assumed we had to have big houses, and the mortgages that go along with them, that we had to live in certain parts of town, and belong to certain clubs. We simply didn't question it.

"Now, when I interview young fellows for the firm, it's a whole different story. You take a top student, from the best school, and what does he ask—'How much vacation do I get? How many hours a day will I need to work?' You can't tell them it's sixteen hours a day, seven days a week, and that they'll get two weeks off if they're lucky. You can't tell them that, because you can't do it to them. They'll go with somebody smaller, they'll go into practice alone, they'll drop the whole thing—but you can't make them give up their lives for the firm. Their wives won't stand for it and they don't want it.

"I wouldn't do it over again," Mark flatly states. "I admire these young people—they've thought things through, whereas we didn't. They've got the right idea."

Mark's wife Celia is also regretful about the years gone by. "I badly wanted more children," she says, "but ours has been a one-parent family so much of the time that I didn't feel I could take on any more responsibility. Now our two children are in their teens, and in a couple of years both of them will be away at college. It was ten or fifteen years ago that it would have meant everything if Mark had slowed down. I blame myself, every bit as much, or more than Mark, for the way we've done things. I followed the pack and just drifted along, seething inside. The truth is that I lacked the guts to let Mark know what kind of family life I really felt we'd all be happier leading."

12

Home Free

A woman can encourage a man toward the human ethic by establishing with him a joint scale of priorities for the style of life they wish to lead. A few fortunate couples evaluate their priorities at the beginning of their marriage, and re-evaluations are frequent; for many others, evaluation begins after the children are born. Whenever a couple begins setting priorities, what is crucial is that each couple decides what is best for them, based on their own desires, personalities, ideals, and life goals, rather than on what they believe is expected of them by parents, teachers, bosses, or peers.

The man who works evenings and weekends because "everybody in the office does it," the woman who chooses to buy a home in a particular locale because others whom she wishes to emulate live there, are insecure in themselves, merely seeking to imitate. Chances are that they're imitating others who are imitating others, none of whom have thought about why they're living as they are, where they are.

In contrast, when a woman evaluates potential life styles with her husband on the basis of what they value for their own lives, and when they continually re-evaluate, they know the *why* of the choices they're making.

When a husband and wife care about one another, they care to spend time with one another. Therefore, they make life-style selections which enable them to have that time. The issues in the lives of couples like the Bradfords, Robertsons, Edams,

Kingsleys, Hastings, and Laffertys are not, "Who *gets* to work and who *has* to stay home and take care of the kids," but rather, "How can we arrange to keep family life first?" . . . "How can we arrange time for both of us to be at home as much as possible?"

Women in families who hold these philosophies share with their husbands the attitude that what an individual does outside the family is one aspect of the self, not the sole definition of the self. Therefore, those women who take on activities in addition to raising their families see their activities as representing merely one dimension of themselves; they run their activities, their activities do not run them.

Similarly, their husbands are not run by their professions or other activities outside the home. These men differ from many of their contemporaries who have similar jobs in one important respect. Each of them has established, with his wife, a set of priorities which allows the family first place in their lives. There is a mutual feeling of importance about the role of the woman within the family, and about the role of the man. Each of these women has a husband who shares her values on the importance of building a close family life, each husband has a wife who's glad she's at home making a home.

Such men insist on time for meals and evenings with the family during the week, for weekends, for holidays and vacations. How do they do it? Sometimes by trading time for money; sometimes by trading time for status; always by establishing and implementing their own priorities, not just following somebody else's. In setting priorities where a couple chooses to make substantial time for their home lives, the location of their home with relation to their other activities—particularly, the man's job—is a crucial factor in determining the total time they have available for family life.

Some families who value their home lives choose to separate home and job completely by distance; others integrate home and work.

SEPARATION OF HOME AND JOB

Where families opt for a complete separation between home and job, they often feel that when a person works he should be "at work" and when he's home, completely home. When that rationale succeeds, it can succeed very well. It usually works best where the man's schedule is predictable; if a man's on a nine-to-five routine over which he has control, he can "turn off" and come home free, evenings and weekends.

Joe Lafferty teaches in an electronics trade school in a program especially designed for culturally disadvantaged youths. Although the Laffertys live more than a half-hour commute from Joe's job headquarters, his hours are predictable. He's gone weekdays, from eight-thirty to five, working in an interesting job in a challenging situation, yet these hours do not conflict with his home life.

Gene and Pat Mattson find living on the outskirts of Tucson, twenty-five minutes from Gene's office, no problem. "We chose this location," Pat says, "because of its physical beauty. We love the outdoors, and this house and location give us the feeling that we're out even when we're in." Gene is an attorney who has "established predictable hours, though others in the firm work at different times. I don't work evenings, except perhaps once or twice a year if something highly unusual comes up. I used to work Saturdays, but I quit doing it. It wasn't worth it; the weather and the countryside are glorious here— that's why we live here. So Pat and I decided we'd keep the weekends for ourselves and the children. I don't want to sit in looking out when I can *be* out." Because Gene has set up a predictable schedule—he is able to work a nine-to-five day, be home for dinner with his family, and be home weekends— neither his job nor commuting to it interferes with his family life.

INTEGRATING HOME AND WORK

More and more families are realizing that when a man's job

hours are unpredictable, living away from his work can cause severe problems in his home that affect his work as well. Some families manage to prevent or solve these problems by integrating a man's work and his home life into one cohesive whole. They do this by erasing the distance between home and job, either by bringing the job home to suburbia—the man offices in the suburb, making of it a small town rather than a bedroom—or if a man's not in a portable profession and works in an urban area, by living in the city.

Many families who choose to live and work away from the city—in suburbs or small towns—who work in offices right in their own homes, or minutes away from them, find plenty of time for family life.

More time for home life is also available to families who have given up suburban living and moved into crowded urban areas; into deteriorating homes in run-down neighborhoods, building them up again; into the already established residential areas, into apartments, sacrificing the space of often-empty homes to be near jobs, and therefore making apartments "people-filled" homes.

In the coming decades many more families are likely to integrate a man's work with his home life so that they can enjoy both, feel pressured by neither. This kind of integration is particularly effective for families where men are in service professions—medicine, clergy—highly "people-centered work." If a man is committed to both a people-centered home and people-centered work, integrating these two elements of his life into a cohesive whole is more effective than trying to separate them, since people never seem to get sick, or to have personal emergencies, between nine and five. Also, living near work serves the needs of many men who are fed up with commuting. These men prefer a more relaxed kind of back-and-forth between home and office; in some cases they office right in their homes.

The advantages to those families who view living and working as part of a whole way of life, as opposed to those where the men have unpredictable work schedules and who have long stretches of freeway between their jobs and their homes, are considerable.

Jim and Rhoda Seeman have particularly impressed me as having freed themselves from the struggle of commuting, juggling personal and work schedules, and who, in so doing, make time for their family life. The Seemans center both his work and her interests at home, though, Rhoda is quick to explain, "We didn't start out this way. Jim went from his residency into a firm of downtown doctors. It meant commuting, and it also meant that while he was 'on duty' he was really on; when he was off, he didn't get called. While this was a boon to some of his colleagues, Jim didn't like it. He takes a deep interest in his patients," Rhoda says with pride. "He didn't really like switching calls with another doctor—he resented not knowing until Monday morning if somebody was seriously ill or injured on his 'off' weekend. He didn't like the commuting, either." The Seemans then lived a half hour out of the city. After heavy evaluation Rhoda and Jim decided "We'd rather have what amounts to a small-town kind of practice. We moved to another suburb and Jim sort of set up his general medicine family practice with the whole family instead of with other doctors. He'll never make as much money, but he's part of our lives, and we're part of his—and his patients are part of our family in a way, too."

Jim and Rhoda have built a large room onto their home for his office-lab. That's where Jim sees "well patients and everyday kind of emergencies which don't require the hospital." According to one of Jim's patients, "That's where he set our daughter's arm one evening minutes after she was hurt . . . his children consoling her all the while. As he finished, Rhoda came down to offer us all cookies. Compare that to waiting for hours in a crowded office or in a hospital emergency room!"

Jim has a phone in his car, so he can be reached anywhere, anytime. He makes rounds in the mornings at a hospital a couple of minutes away from his home, makes house calls for his young patients when mothers ask him to see sore throats, painful ears, high fevers. "I culture every suspicious-looking throat and can do that in their homes as well as in the office," Jim says. "I find there's little rationale for bringing a sick child out, except for the doctor's convenience. You can always have the child come in if, after seeing him at home, you feel it's necessary, but usually it's run-of-the-mill viral stuff, or a bacterial infection that shows in the throat culture and will respond to a drug. You can tell that at home."

Jim has limited his practice to the suburb in which he lives. He and one other doctor (who also practices from home) take care of most of the families "in town." No patient lives more than a five-minute drive from Jim's home and that, he feels, is what makes his way of practicing unique.

"When a patient moves to another suburb, though it's often hard on us both, I recommend another doctor who lives near them," Jim says. "If I had to spend fifteen or twenty minutes each way to see a case, I couldn't do justice to them or myself. I'd wind up doing a lot by phone. That's no good for anyone."

Because Jim has such a flexible schedule he and Rhoda often play golf on spring and summer afternoons (he has a radiophone in his pocket, leaves the course to see a patient when necessary). Jim leads a cub scout troop and is part of a community drama group.

Rhoda handles the phone a good share of the time from her studio, which adjoins Jim's home office. Rhoda began painting when she left her med-tech job to have their first baby. "I love to paint, but I don't give it much time. When the children are older I'll take serious lessons, but right now I paint to relax. We have a busy family life, and I also like helping Jim with the phone and the patients. It takes a load off him, and makes more total time for all of us."

The Seeman's life style provides a refreshing contrast to the kind of rat race in which many professionals find themselves. Nobody knows that better than Jim Seeman. "My goal is neither wealth nor fame," Jim grins. "My aim is to take care of sick people, and keep well people well; besides that I like time for my hobbies, and for the family to grow together. By my standards, we're very rich!"

Other families choose to live in crowded urban areas in order to combine their work with their family life. Rebecca and Sam Edam moved into Baltimore "just about the time it was becom-

ing 'the thing' for others with families to get out. We figured
there are all kinds of survival and if we were to survive as a
family we'd better be able to spend time together. We could
more easily move into the city than move Sam's office into our
suburb, so that's just what we did. We've survived, physically;
the children are in public school; I'm working part-time on an
advanced degree in history. We are able to spend dinnertime,
evenings and weekends as a family, things we couldn't easily do
when Sam was commuting. For instance, when Sam has an
out-of-town client, he doesn't take him to dinner in a restaurant, but brings him home, instead. This works out beautifully
now that we live in town. All in all, we're delighted with our ar-
rangement."

Another couple who integrate their work and family life are
Ray and Lee Harnes, who own a family store in the midst of a
sprawling eastern city, and live around the corner from their
store. After college graduation, Ray worked for a year in a large
food chain before going into the service. That was in 1941.
"After the war, I was offered a job comparable to the one I'd
left. But I'd done some thinking overseas, and I didn't see
spending my life working for somebody else. Lee and I were
married just before I went into the service; we were anxious to
start a family, so the company job would have meant instant
security. But we took a chance on something else instead."

Lee, his blue-eyed wife, laughingly remembers—"It seems
like yesterday that Ray got out of the service and we used his
mustering-out pay for a down payment on our store." The "ma
and pa" grocery store—known to everyone in the neighborhood
as Ray and Lee's—is a throwback to the corner grocery of yes-
teryear. By all odds it should have folded before 1945, rather
than beginning then. The tiny, old-fashioned market is open six
days a week from eight-thirty to six-thirty and "by appointment." (An emergency call to Ray—"We've got company and
I forgot to buy coffee when I was in this morning"—will bring
him to the door with the coffee; "Would you open up; we're
out of milk?" will have him at the store to meet you before you
get there.)

I asked Ray why he doesn't stay open longer hours. "We can't compete with the twenty-four-hour supermarkets anyway," Ray says. "I'd rather just close and go home for supper. People don't call all that often, and when they do I'm glad to oblige. One of the kids and I hustle over and help them out."

Lee works in the store, too—"more now than I used to before our three children were grown. I love to see people I know, and meet new ones." When the children were small, "I went in an hour or two a day, a neighbor stayed with the kids during their naps. She'd call me when they got up or dress them and bring them in. They knew many of the customers' names almost as soon as they knew ours."

Jim and Rhoda Seeman, Rebecca and Sam Edam, and Ray and Lee Harnes are but a few of the increasing number of persons who have chosen to integrate their home lives with their work and other activities. Though each has implemented the theme of integrating home and work differently, making the two parts of their lives into one complementary whole is their common goal. What they really share, and what may be worth while noting for all of us who complain about the complexities and vastness of modern life is this: each person has managed to bring some old-fashioned "small townness" to his and her daily life. While each may have fewer total human contacts than in a larger setting, each is able to interact more closely with them. The customer, the business contact, the patient is more than a commodity. As Rhoda Seeman says, "They're part of the family, really."

In my own experience, I've found a home where work and family life are integrated an ideal kind of home in which to grow up and in which to raise our own family.

I was raised on the grounds of a state mental hospital in Hastings, Minnesota. When my father, who served as the hospital's psychiatrist-director, was given the choice of a home in town or one on the grounds of the hospital, he opted for the latter. As a devoted father and husband, he didn't want us living any further from his work than necessary; as a committed doctor he didn't want to live any further from his patients than he had to. Patients, and their own relatives, hospital employees, staff and visiting doctors were in our home a great deal; and as children, my sister and I benefited tremendously from knowing these persons and from being a part of my father's dedication to help others.

My father was an advocate of the right of each patient to be treated with dignity and respect. Therefore when he took over the superintendency of the Hastings hospital in the late 1930s, he made major changes in the existing system. The most radical of these advances was his insistence that all patients be unshackled, and that non-restraint methods of care and treatment be instituted. Ranking closely with his removing restraint was his stopping the double mealtime standard, where the staff ate well-prepared foods in a relaxing atmosphere, while hurried employees slopped unpalatable food onto patients' plates. As soon as one menu and one dining hall became the rule for staff and patients alike, the patients' diet and eating conditions quickly improved.

My dad knew each of his 1,100 patients by their first names. My mother, my sister Ricky, and I knew many of them, too, and spent considerable time with some of them. In fact, our home was a kind of "halfway house" years before the concept of such houses as a means of rehabilitating and gradually reacclimating a mentally ill person into the larger society came into acceptance in this country.

Often, one or more patients lived with us for a period of time before going out on their own. I particularly remember Larry, who slept on the third floor, and who played gin rummy with me by the hour; Amanda, who slept in the back guest room, and wrote poetry which she used to share with Ricky and me; and Carl and Greg, both of whom lived in the walkout basement level of our house during the day, and slept in one of the hospital buildings at night. Carl, who liked to garden, helped Ricky and me plant and nourish carrots, peas, and beans, from the time we could walk. Greg, who had a vast knowledge of history, was a repository of all sorts of information on generals, battles, and kings. But once in a while he'd get a message from "the underground" and become worried.

Then he couldn't talk about much else, except the message and what it portended. Sometimes Greg wanted Daddy to send these messages to the President, so Ricky and I would hurry to ask him to get word to Washington. Once we'd assured Greg that the President would get his news, he would relax again, and tell us more tales of history.

The most agile skater on our back-yard ice-skating rink was a gentle man, a patient named Jim, who had been mute for over thirty years. Although he didn't speak, he often helped Ricky and me skate, and when we asked, he'd demonstrate figure eights for us. Once, when Ricky was trying to emulate him, she fell on the ice and shrieked in pain. Jim skated to her in a flash, scooped her into his arms, and comforted her, saying, "There, there, you'll be fine." The sound of his voice startled her so that she stopped crying, but the moment she did he put her down, skated away, and to the best of my knowledge hasn't spoken since.

Our family frequently spent holidays in ways which at the time seemed perfectly natural to me, but which, in retrospect, I realize to have been a bit unusual. For instance, every Fourth of July the Hastings State Hospital hosted a picnic for the young men from the Red Wing Training School (then Minnesota's state reformatory for males under twenty-one). Ricky and I always looked forward to watching the annual baseball game in which the patients played against the boys from the reform school, and to eating a delicious picnic supper afterward with our patients and the Red Wing contingent.

Clearly, my mother, sister, and I felt a part of my father's work because our lives were intertwined with it. Similarly, I've always felt very much a part of Dick's work. In fact, I once startled a number of women at a Harvard newcomers' tea, when I was asked how I liked the school, and I replied matter-of-factly, "Being at Harvard is so much like living in a mental hospital." I had to hasten to explain that living practically in Harvard Yard and having students and faculty all around made me feel the same sense of belonging to what my husband was doing, as I had to what my father did.

I've felt particularly close to Dick's work since we've been back at Minnesota, which is my alma mater. We live an easy walk to and from the University of Minnesota main campus, and having students, their families, and their friends in our home is a matter of course. Consequently, my sense of identification with Dick's work is very positive. Although it's become unfashionable in some circles today for a woman to feel a part of her husband's work, such a sense of identification is essential. When one partner in a marriage cannot feel a part of the activities of the other—but feels either indifference or antipathy—both the marriage and the activities suffer. Conversely, when one partner feels a part of what the other does, both the relationship and the activities are enhanced. In our own case, just as I'm involved with Dick's activities, he is very much a part of mine. I rely on his help and encouragement; he gives me constructive criticism, is proud of me when things go well, and commiserates with me when they don't. If he didn't support my endeavors with his enthusiasm and energy, it would ruin the fun.

When one has an activity that's enjoyable, and worth doing, it's happiest if everyone involved feels a part of it. What a person *does*—in terms of a job—is really only one more aspect of his or her total self. When one learns to do one's job in such a way that it is integrated into one's total life—the result is not only happier family lives, but happier personal lives as well.

Conclusion
Hopes, Dreams, Prophecies

Yesterday, staying at home to raise a family was a woman's destiny; today it is her choice. Tomorrow, every woman at home will have strong reasons for her decision. One of her goals will be the creation of a secure, close-knit family life; another will be the development of her personal resources.

The woman at home of tomorrow will be either self-educated or formally educated, and frequently will have specific training in a profession. She will, in the span of forty or fifty years of marriage, contribute at various times to the family income. This contribution may take the form of savings from work before marriage, or from the early years of working before children are born. It may come from work she will do after her family is raised, or from some kind of part-time work she does at home.

The woman at home of tomorrow will find that her time allows her to discover and to develop various aspects of her self in new ways. She will enjoy the independence of doing her own thing, to her own specifications, according to her own timetable, without sacrificing her family to do so.

Women and men who choose to marry will marry with a clearer idea of their hopes, dreams, and ideals than when the social norm was "marry—you'll all like it." Matching goals—before marriage—will be part of their future planning. A woman who visualizes herself jetting to Paris for a business conference (hers not his) will not seek to marry a man who pictures himself sitting by the fire with children clamoring 'round as his wife plays the piano nearby. Similarly, a woman who wishes not only to marry and have children, but to create a warm, secure family life, will seek to match goals with a man who shares her values.

The woman of the family of the future will encourage her husband to be a full participant in family life. The result will be the kind of family in which the adult members value human relationships more than the status or money that exclusive dedication to one's function outside home might bring.

The man who elects marriage and family in the future will be a man who enjoys his work. But in contrast to those men who pursue the success ethic to the exclusion of personal relationships and development, he will work to live rather than live to work. He will be a man who values the closeness and warmth of his family more than the ego gratification he might derive from more time on the job.

Curiously, feminism, which frees women for the success ethic, also has contributed to freeing both women and men from its snare. In forcing choices, assessments of priorities and values, feminism clarifies the fact that pursuit of material success requires time, energy, and a single-mindedness of purpose which frequently precludes all else.

Women and men will enter the next millennium divided. But the dichotomy will be based on value systems rather than on anatomy. Women and men who wish to pursue the success ethic will be free to do so, without the social pressure to marry and have children. Women and men who prefer to place human relationships over material matters will be free to pursue a human ethic without being owned by their jobs and job labels. Instead, they will be free to share and experience life with those human beings who matter most to them.